# The 12 Keys to
# SPIRITUAL
# VITALITY

# The 12 Keys to SPIRITUAL VITALITY

## Powerful Lessons on Living Agelessly

### RICHARD P. JOHNSON, PH.D.

Liguori

LIGUORI, MISSOURI

Published by Liguori Publications
Liguori, Missouri
www.liguori.org

**Library of Congress Cataloging-in-Publication Data**

Johnson, Richard P.
    The 12 keys to spiritual vitality : powerful lessons on living age-
lessly / Richard P. Johnson. — 1st ed.
      p.  cm.
    ISBN 978-0-7648-0230-0
    1. Aging—Religious aspects—Christianity.  I. Title.
BV4580.J64  1998                        98-26655
248.8'5—dc21

Liguori Publications, a nonprofit corporation, is an apostolate of the
Redemptorists. To learn more about the Redemptorists, visit *Redemp-
torists.com.*

Printed in the United States of America
12 11 10   10 9 8

## To Professor Emeritus Harold C. Riker (deceased)

For four years, Dr. Riker was my major professor at the University of Florida. As head of my doctoral committee, Dr. Riker served as my mentor in the fullest sense of the word. He guided my thinking and my goals and added considerably to the vision of aging that would eventually propel me to write this book.

I have deep and lasting gratitude for Harold Riker: he was a man of principle, a man of generosity, dedication, and compassion. Above all, however, Harold Riker was always a committed Christian who lived out his faith every day of his life. Thank you.

# Contents

# Introduction

---

# The 12 Keys of Agelessness

This is a book on how to become ageless, or spiritually vital. Actually, the main tenet of this book is that you already are ageless, yet most of us don't know what that means, nor how to tap into this agelessness that lives deep within us. Some people say that aging is only an attitude. If this is true at any level, then we could conclude that youth-fulness—or what I prefer to call agelessness—is also an attitude.

This book is a short course on spiritual vitality and the attitudes of agelessness, and how to make them work for you in your aging process. To do this, you must discard what you already believe about aging and the process we call maturation and take on an entirely new mind-set.

As you read the next paragraph, develop an image in your mind's eye of the person it describes.

### There She Lay

There she lay in her bed, still, as I watch her sleeping. My thoughts turn to questions: Why, God, cannot she speak? Why can't she think rational thoughts? Why is her mind so weak so that no meaningful cognition emerges from it? Her eyes are insensitive now, her muscles weak. She has no stamina and is now completely dependent upon her caregivers for everything. She can't feed herself; she is incontinent of urine and bowel. No fine motor skills has she, no sense of taste. Indeed, all of her senses are dim now. She drools and she whines; tears occasionally roll down her cheeks. She seems generally unable to care for herself in any way. She appears helpless. She is disoriented as to person, place, and time. She seems to have no sense of her own existential presence. She appears uncomfortable, fearful, and without purpose or personal direction.

What image emerged when you read this description? Who is this person just described? Since this book is subtitled *Powerful Lessons on Living Agelessly,* it's natural for you to have imagined a frail older woman, perhaps in a nursing-home bed, perhaps even in a semi-fetal position because of an advanced dementia, maybe even Alzheimer's disease. You probably imagined wrinkles and gray hair, dimmed eyes, and an inability to communicate, among other physical diminishments.

The feelings that you experienced as you brought this image to mind were probably feelings of compassion, fear, hopelessness, perhaps even disgust. Also feelings of pity for her, for somehow this poor woman had encountered debilitating difficulties in her life and was now enthroned, almost entombed, in this bed that will be her final resting place in this world.

Many people have such images when they read this paragraph. It is not, however, a description of an old, feeble, and demented woman; on the contrary, I wrote it to describe a two-and-a-half-*week*-old female infant. Doesn't that change your perspective and make you pause to think about how we normally conceive of this process called aging? We seem immediately to move into a thought pattern that says to us, "Isn't this too bad?" Our culture reveres youth, so we're prone to thinking that things that are young are better—and, by contrast, that things that are not so young are not quite so good, or are even "too bad."

## Aging: The Thief in the Night?

I remember, while I was producing a training videotape on caring for aging parents, interviewing a woman in her eighty-third year. She was of Irish descent, and she was relating a conversation she had had with her son. She said, "I was talking to my son, Jim, the other day. I said, 'Jim, I went to church last Sunday, and you know the church was packed with old people.' My son, Jim, says to me, 'Well, Mother, what do you think you are?'"

She shot up in her chair right there on the videotape and held her hand to her forehead and said, "I never thought of that. I never thought of myself as being old." She continued, "I always thought I was...." She didn't know how to finish the sentence. She couldn't find the right words to describe her astonishment at her son's response. She tried again, "I thought I was...." Once again, she was befuddled and puzzled as to how to finish the sentence. Finally, on the third try she said, "I thought I was...all right."

I think the statement of this beautiful elder woman sums

up for us what our culture feels and thinks about this thing called aging, that aging isn't "all right." By extension, our culture feels there's something wrong with the very process of aging. That somehow we shouldn't be doing it!

Are you not doing it? Of course you are; we all are! The life process tells us that we must do it, and that we do it every day.

We know we're aging when we get up every morning and look in the mirror and say, "Something happened last night, because I don't look the same. Somewhere there was a thief that took something from me last night, and I don't like it."

Psychiatrists have a name for people who think one thing and yet profess something quite different through their behavior. They say this person has a *thought disorder.* In extreme cases, they would say, this person suffers from schizophrenia. In our culture we are all somewhat schizophrenic about aging. At the very least, we suffer from a double standard about aging. We possess confusing, confounding, and altogether puzzling ideas about what this thing called aging is all about. We don't know what it is; indeed, we are afraid of it.

## A Plan for Healthy Aging

I learned a tremendous amount while pursuing my degree in gerontology at the University of Florida. I learned much more, however, in my many years of clinical experience with aging persons and their families. This book distills this knowledge and experience into a plan for healthy aging, a plan that involves your body, your mind, and your spirit.

This book actually emerged from an important question

I couldn't seem to escape. For fifteen years I worked in a large hospital where I saw many patients, a good majority of whom were "older." I stood shoulder to shoulder with their physicians every day in my professional life. I looked at and studied elder people who came in with physical ailments of all kinds. What puzzled me was that there seemed to be two distinct groups. Some of them were chronologically quite old, perhaps ninety-five years of age, but looked and acted as if they were thirty years younger. Others who came in were chronologically only forty-five or fifty years old but who looked and acted as if they had been here for ninety-five years.

Now, I don't like using these chronological demarcators called age, because age doesn't mean much; I think we overvalue our age. Your age—that number that you think is tattooed to your forehead for all to see, clicking higher like an odometer every year at your birthday—means only the number of times you've circumnavigated the sun. But as I looked at these people in the hospital, I asked myself, "What are the differences between the person who's been here for ninety-five years and acts forty-five, and the person who is forty-five yet acts ninety-five?" I felt compelled to study this phenomenon.

With my scientific cap on, I started observing personality qualities in order to gain some insight into this perplexing question. I observed many characteristics that seemed to be *keys to spiritual vitality,* or agelessness, or youthfulness. Call it what you will. Over the years my list grew longer and longer. After four years of study, I had collected forty-three different characteristics that defined for me the difference between what could be seen as ageless behavior and what was clearly "old" behavior—forty-three qualities that separated ageless person A from aged person B. Ageless Joseph is vital, alive, but it was hard to even conceive that aged Josephine had ever been a child. You know the kind of people I mean: he's perpetually blooming, while she comes down her mother's birth canal and she's already old. I have nothing against something that's old, and I'm not trying to deny age. As a matter of fact, I like age, and I look forward to the days when I will be older. I think age is a necessary part of God's plan. We need to understand aging in that way. God brought us aging as a gift. I will define that much more clearly as we proceed. But I never want to act "old." I never want to act as though I've lost my agelessness, or my youthfulness, or my vitality.

## Youthfulness

We don't want to confuse the word "youthfulness" with youth. I once attended a very large gerontology conference at which a well-known gerontologist was speaking. He opened the keynote address of the conference with a reference to Alcoholics Anonymous, announcing to the thousand people before him, "Let me introduce myself: my name is Tom; I'm a recovering youth." His quip sums up for us the truth that indeed there is something to recover from in youth, and underscores for me the fact that the maturation process, particularly in one's later years, has potential for personal, character, and most of all spiritual development far beyond what we formerly thought. I believe that more growth can take place in one's later years than in any other time of life!

I believe that to be youthful you must be very mature and that the forty-three qualities I had observed were actually behavioral signs of maturation. But how did the maturation process turn into this thing called "aging"? I see maturation as incremental, increasing, additive; I see aging—getting "old"—as decremental, decreasing, discounting. It's a matter of attitudes, and we have to change ours.

I decided that forty-three qualities was too many. I compacted the list of forty-three into twenty. Using these twenty, I gave several seminars in local retirement centers and hospitals. I found that twenty was still too many. Once again I compacted the list, this time into the twelve keys I present in this book.

## The 12 Keys to Spiritual Vitality

Here are the twelve keys:

1. Transform your attitudes about maturation.
2. Seek love everywhere.
3. Delight in connectedness.
4. Live in the now.
5. Accept your true self.
6. Forgive others and self.
7. Let go of anger and other inner turmoil.
8. Give of yourself to others.
9. Celebrate your faith.
10. Discover the deep meaning in your life.
11. Make your feelings work for you.
12. Achieve balance in your life.

These twelve keys are the result of much study, research, and clinical experience, and I assure you, the degree to which

you can incorporate them into your lifestyle will be the degree
to which you will maximize your God-given growth potential. With these twelve, you will let your unique light shine,
becoming more yourself, more the person that God intended
you to be. You will be youthful, no matter what your age.

## Tending Our Garden

I like to use the metaphor of a garden to illustrate the tender
care with which we need to treat ourselves. A gardener's
first job is to tend the soil. Gardeners cherish the soil; they
let it sift through their fingers with great gratitude; they
cultivate it, nourish it, water it, and keep it free from weeds
and other pests. Why does a gardener do this? When the
soil is fertile, it accepts the seed into its gentle embrace.
The seed finds there the best possible environment for maximum growth, the place where God's power can infuse that
seed with life. The gardener doesn't make the tomatoes
grow, or the roses grow, or the marigolds grow; only God
provides the power for that. The gardener merely ensures
that the environment is as conducive to growth as possible.

You too have a garden. It's the garden of your soul, and
it's your job to tend your garden well. When you tend your
spiritual garden well, your spirituality can drink in God's
life-power, which infuses spirit and vitality into you so that
you can grow abundantly.

Our job in life is to tend our spiritual garden well. How
do we do that? By using the twelve keys or tools of spiritual vitality and "agelessness." The keys are like the hoes,
rakes, and watering cans that you would need to tend a
flower or vegetable garden. If we use these twelve keys
well, we will be able to harvest the high-quality fruits of

emotional and spiritual growth throughout our elder years. The better you incorporate these twelve keys into your everyday living, the better prepared you will be to harvest God's abundance from the garden of your life.

I'm glad you've found this book, and I hope that you read it through, because as you do you will realize that you are embarking on a new adventure. This book unfolds a whole new way of living, a whole new perspective on this thing called aging, something that you do every single day of your life and something that our culture is telling you not to do.

Have you ever seen pro-wrinkle cream? No, because our culture doesn't understand aging, it doesn't understand the benefits and gifts that aging has to offer. By the time you finish this book, you'll be glad you're moving along the maturation process, because the alternative is not death, it's personal and spiritual stagnation, a kind of walking woundedness, a forlorn brokenness that means simply surviving in your world...not thriving.

# The 12 Keys to SPIRITUAL VITALITY

# Key 1

---

# Transform Your Attitudes about Maturation

*You were taught to put away your former way of life, your old self, corrupt and deluded by its lusts, and to be renewed in the spirit of your minds, and to clothe yourselves with the new self, created according to the likeness of God in true righteousness and holiness.*

Ephesians 4:22–24

**Key 1 Definition:** The degree to which you have successfully shifted your basic beliefs about aging from beliefs involving loss to beliefs involving heightened opportunity for spiritual development.

The definition of Key 1 is a somewhat formal way of saying that for us to really understand aging the way God wants us to—to truly grasp the vitalizing significance of the maturation process—we must first transform our attitudes about aging.

Let's take a look at the word *transform*. The prefix *trans*

1

means "to go beyond, to go over, to go across." The word *form* refers to all things that are physical, material, of this world. *Transform* means to go beyond the physical.

All physical things have form. Things that are not physical do not have form. The very first key to spiritual vitality, the number one thing we need to do to become ageless in the Lord, is to *transform* our attitudes and get beyond the physical plane in our perspective on aging.

## Why Does God Allow Aging?

Have you ever thought, "Why does aging occur? Why does God allow something so destructive as aging?" If aging were brought before the highest court of the land, or were brought up for a vote before the populace, do you think it would be allowed? No way! But God allows it. Why?

If God allows aging to exist, it must have a purpose. What is this process of aging all about? What are we supposed to think about it? Why must we endure all the pain and loss that seem to be part and parcel of the process of getting off this planet? Wouldn't it be easier not to go through this kind of thing?

Perhaps there's a better question to ask: When did the process of maturation, which we see as a positive force, become the thief in the night that we see as aging? This question gets to the heart of the matter: our own attitudes.

## Attitudes about Aging

Your attitudes are the mother of all your actions. Before anything moves toward action, it must first be an attitude. It must then be converted into a perception, then into a thought, then through your feelings into a decision, and finally into an action. Attitudes are everything because nothing can happen without first being an attitude. Your current attitudes define your present life: what you perceive and think, what you decide, and what you do. What you believe about yourself will come to be. Change your attitudes and you will change your life! So it's clear that what you believe about aging—what your *attitudes* are about aging—will become clearly reflected in your life as you mature.

Collectively, our attitudes about aging are pretty negative. We seem to suffer from a prejudice against the later phases of life. This prejudice is called *ageism.* Other cultures don't suffer from ageism in quite the same ways that we do, but our culture seems particularly confused about the purpose of aging, perhaps because we have such a forthright, can-do kind of spirit, which seems to favor the younger years. These attitudes are irrational, yet they persist in so many forms.

Aging challenges us to remember that God uses our natural human condition as a teaching aid so that we can better learn the power of God's love ever more personally. Aging is not a contradiction of God's promise of abundance; rather, it is an extension of that promise. Aging allows us to live in abundance. For us to benefit from this promise of abundance, we must learn to celebrate our own aging as a valuable process of growth and development, not berate it as a senseless slippage into nothingness. We can irreparably damage our well-being when we live out the later years of life with attitudes prejudiced against aging.

## We Are Called to See Aging Differently

The world sees aging merely as a succession of losses. The world sees aging as a painful descent into nothingness, as a senseless slippage of strength, as a loss of stature, sensitivity, security.

How often do you watch TV? How often do you listen to the radio? How often do you read the newspaper or other news magazines? Most of us do these every day. Every day that you hear an advertisement on the radio, or see a commercial on TV, or read an ad in the newspaper, you are encountering *the* worldly message. No matter what they're selling in that ad, whether it's automobiles or toothpaste or financial security, the undergirding message is the same, and it's very simple: "You are your body—your body alone and nothing else. You are form."

Here is what the world believes you are and nothing more: form. The world is of form, and that's all it can see. Worldliness means focusing on the form. In truth, we can't expect anything more from the world because the world is form, it is from form, and it can only deal on the form level.

How does the commercial world or culture see aging as form? It sees aging only as wrinkles, gray hair or loss of hair, stooped gait, dimmed eyes, inability to do the 100-yard dash in 9.8 seconds anymore, inability to bound those steps like you used to when you were younger, and so on. The commercial culture sees aging as something bad, something that will only take away from you.

The degree to which you adopt this worldly view of aging is the degree to which you will age poorly. Your definition of aging will be the same as the world's: a succession of losses, a painful descent into nothingness, a senseless slippage of strength. If all you are is your body, then what does aging do to you? It comes to take your body away, and when your body is taken away, according to the world's definition of aging, then *you* are taken away.

The world is blind to truth, beauty, and goodness, and that applies to aging too. Christians are called to see aging from a vantage point dramatically different from that of the non-Christian world. This is why Jesus reminded us, "Give therefore to the emperor the things that are the emperor's, and to God the things that are God's." So we are called in Key 1 to be transformed. We as Christians cannot see aging simply in terms of *form*.

Ask yourself, "Are you your body?" Do we as people of faith believe that that's what we are, a body? No! Our body is part of us on this plane. Our body is where our spiritual nature resides on this plane. Our body is the way we communicate with others on this plane. Your body is in this world *and* also of it. What happens on Ash Wednesday? We receive ashes on our forehead and are reminded, "Remember you are dust and to dust you shall return." What's being talked about here? Certainly not our spiritual entity. It's our form. As Jesus told us, we are "…in this world but not of it."

When we are stuck in seeing aging only through our "form" eyes, we have a problem. We need to see aging through Jesus' eyes. We need to put on a whole new pair of eyes if we are to understand aging at all! God wants the best for us. God gave us strong bodies to do God's work here on this plane; it's these bodily changes that call us back to our real home. All of us are orphans on this earth, and we really want to go home.

Freud even said this. He said all of us want to go back to our mother's womb. He had the right idea, only he had the wrong place!

A simple story may illustrate this point. The story is about a very good Christian man who dies and goes to heaven. He gets to the "pearly gates" of heaven and stands before Saint Peter.

Saint Peter says, "Welcome, my man, it's good to have you here. You were God's faithful servant all the days of your life."

"Well," says the man, "I'm very glad to be here, but I've got a bone to pick with God. I'd like to talk to God."

Saint Peter, in his humility, goes to get God. Very soon thereafter God comes down the celestial path and says, "Yes, my son, welcome to heaven. What can I do for you?"

The man says, "I did everything to work in the vineyards for you, but we've got a problem. Lord, I've got to tell you you're making a mistake down there. And I'm not the only person who thinks this way; everybody else does too. Go take a poll of at any church, and 99 percent of them think just like me. We've got to shake this thing down."

"Yes, my son," says God, "go on."

"Well, God," continues the man, "you gave me this body, this wonderful body. It's a miracle that even medical science can't completely figure out—how this marvelous body works—it works so well, so beautifully. Every year of my life, Lord, you made this body better. Every year you made it stronger. Every year you made it more supple. Every year you made it smarter and more sensitive and able to do more and more. That was, of course, until I was about twenty-five."

The man goes on, "That's the crux of my problem, Lord, because after that time why did you, Lord, every single year of my life, take something away from my body? At first, imperceptibly, you took a little strength, a little stamina;

you took a little suppleness, a little flexibility, a little bright-
ness in my eyes, and more and more of my hair. What are
you doing, Lord? I don't understand this. Why did you give
this body to me only to take it away? Do you realize that if
you had left me with the body of a twenty-five-year-old
what I could have done in your vineyards?

"Do you realize," asks the man, "that when I was twenty-
five I hardly needed four hours of sleep a night? I could go-
go-go and never stop. What's this thing called 'aging,' Lord?
We don't like it. It doesn't work. It doesn't help build up
the Church. We've got to do something about aging, Lord.

"I've got a good idea," proceeds the man. "Lord, we can
solve this whole problem of aging by one simple stroke.
Allow people to grow and mature until they reach about
twenty-five years of age. Then, simply let them stop growing. They could live sixty, seventy, even eighty more years
on earth before you called them home. They would live
their life in a twenty-five-year-old body. Think of all the
work that could be done in the vineyards, Lord! Think of
all the good that could be accomplished. People would understand you better too, Lord! It would be better all the way
around!"

After a long pause the Lord says, "My son...I love you.
I couldn't love you more. The love I have for you surpasses
all understanding that you could ever have. I want you to
know that I gave you the *gift* of aging; yes, my son, the *gift*
of aging, so that you wouldn't take the fake of the world. I
wanted you to understand, proof positive, without doubt,
no questions asked—I wanted you to know who you are. I
wanted you to know clearly that you were *in* the world that
I created, but that you were not *of* it. If I didn't give you the
gift of aging, your life would make little sense, because

you would take the fake of the world. You would come to believe that you were your body and nothing else, that you were not who you really are. I gave you aging so you would know who you really are. I love you that much!"

This story is simple, but the message is important. Aging is not a thief in the night; it is your *master teacher*. Aging teaches you life lessons like nothing else can. Let's look at this more closely.

## Necessary Losses

Even when we look at aging simply from a human perspective, we can learn to see it differently. A skilled author, Judith Viorst, wrote a wonderful book titled *Necessary Losses,* which brings the reader through the whole life span, from birth to death. The central tenet of the book is something incredible: You grow only when you lose. This is a startling assertion!

I had always conceived of growth as something additive, or incremental, a process that makes one bigger, better. How can growth come only when you lose? The idea seems ridiculous, yet Viorst maintains that the primary motive force of growth on this plane is loss. Without loss, you can't grow. I had to think about this for a long time before it finally started to make some sense.

Perhaps the best way to understand is to ask a question. Can you remember when you were a toddler? Were you ever a toddler? You probably were. What happened to your toddlerhood? In Judith Viorst's words, you lost it. You lost your toddlerhood. When did you lose your toddlerhood? You lost it just before you crossed the bridge into childhood. As a matter of fact, Viorst would say, you couldn't have crossed the bridge, you couldn't even have opened the door to the next developmental stage of life called childhood unless you first gave up—unless you lost—toddlerhood. We don't get into childhood and then lose toddlerhood; we must lose toddlerhood first. Once we give up, or lose, toddlerhood, we then have the opportunity to move on into childhood. And every life stage works the same way, requiring loss in order to gain.

If loss is the primary force of growth on this plane, when is the time of life when the most growth is possible? The answer, of course, is when we experience the most loss. Generally, people lose the most from their lives during their later years. So we can conclude that the later years have more growth potential than any other time of life. So if we fully understood aging, we would welcome it with open arms as the most "growthful" time in our life. Does our culture understand this? Do we have any inkling of how fantastic this is for us as a society, as a culture, as a people? Not at this time, but times are changing!

## The Paradox of Aging and Our Emerging Spirituality

The growth that aging brings is internal growth, but we've become so focused on the form of life that we forget what growth is really all about. Growth takes place internally, spiritually, psychologically, emotionally; growth is character development, personality development, spiritual development. This is all internal growth. In our later years, the true drama of our life unfolds in the arenas of personality development and spiritual development. The world can't see this kind of growth: growth in understanding, growth in wisdom, growth in peace. In the later phases of our lives, the gain is spiritual.

Aging is chock-full of "growthful diminishments," "harmonizing disintegration," and "peace-giving chaos." These phrases sound self-contradictory, but they illustrate the marvelous spiritual paradox of aging.

Without question, the elder years bring physical diminishments in ways quite different from previous stages. These diminishments are more frequent, last longer, and are more life-disturbing as compared to what has come before. Paradoxically, it is precisely because of these diminishments that we become capable of heightened growth. Hence, we experience "growthful diminishments."

As we mature (at least past age twenty-five), the process of physical disintegration seems relentless. It become a continuous struggle to keep our bodies in good shape. Eventually, regardless of our heroic efforts at trying to stem the tide, aging always wins. Yet throughout this process we are never called, or forced, or coerced to become "old." Certainly, we mature, we age, we change: this is the imperative of all things physical. "Oldness," however, is not of the body, but of the mind and the spirit. As our bodies disintegrate, we ourselves—our true selves—become more clearly and fully integrated, become more comfortably who we are. This is the paradox of "harmonizing disintegration."

Finally, aging can be chaotic, calling us to deal with increasing ambiguity. In each arena of our life we are called to abandon ideas, beliefs, convictions, and attitudes that have sustained us in earlier stages, and to replace them with new ones. Old ideas are antiques of our mind that only impede our growthful progression in the elder years. All of this is chaotic indeed! Yet we are called in our elder years to see such chaos as peace. How paradoxical, that shifting one's whole frame of reference—shifting one's attitudes about aging away from the form dimension and into God's eternal dimension—can be peace-giving.

George Eastman, founder of the Eastman Kodak Company, took his life several months after his retirement. In his last note he wrote, "My work is finished, why wait?" Here is the stark ending of the life of a gifted man who, although he was sick, couldn't find the beautiful paradox of aging. He couldn't see anything positive for him in his later years; he couldn't see his life with new eyes. He ended the chaos he felt by doing what he had always done, taking his life into his own hands.

Losses are not tragedies; they're not something to lament. Losses are opportunities leading us closer to the fulfillment of knowing God. Growth in Christ is a progression of losses and gains: the loss of worry and the gain of trust; the loss of fear and the gain of confidence; the loss of resentment and the gain of forgiveness; the loss of ill will and the gain of love. Anything is blessed when it brings us closer to God, and that includes aging. The blessed paradoxes of aging become our pathways to a vital spirituality.

## The Doorknob

Each of the keys has a symbol that captures its essence. The symbol for the first key is a doorknob. To genuinely enter into the true meaning of our elder years, we must open new doors to our soul. We do this by developing new ideas and attitudes about the very purpose of aging.

Perhaps even more important is the fact that maturation constantly calls us to close doors too. The doors we must

close are to those rooms in our mind where we keep former
definitions of ourselves. We cannot bring these former
identities along with us; "agelessness" requires that we
experience the loss of our "old" selves before we can
grow, before we can become new.

# Key 2

---

# Seek Love Everywhere

*Beloved, let us love one another, because love is from God; everyone who loves is born of God and knows God.*

1 John 4:7

**Key 2 Definition:** The degree to which we strive to find God's presence, however remotely, in everything and in everyone.

The second key to spiritual vitality is to seek love everywhere. No, I'm not kidding! We *are* called by our Christian faith to seek love everywhere. Jesus told us that in every place we walk, with each person we encounter, in every situation we experience, we are to ask the question *Where is the love here?* The world, of course, sees such behavior as ridiculous, even a bit nutty. People of the world would say that your head was in the clouds, and your feet were not on the ground, because the world would assert that love is *not* everywhere. Many would argue that there are plenty of places where only the absence of love, or the shadow of love, exists.

The world tells us that we must seek security and protect ourselves. The world says, "Here, take this glass of water, you can have it, you can drink it. But when you do drink it, you don't have it anymore, the water is gone. And if I give my glass of water to you, then I don't have it any longer." This is the way the world works, but it is not the way love works. When we put self-protection at center stage in our life, we buffer ourselves from love as well. Love functions in exactly the opposite way from the world's approach. What did Jesus teach us? Love is the most abundant thing in the universe. The more you give away love, the more you get it back. If I give you love, I simply get more love in return.

Jesus gave us the admonition to love: love God, love our neighbors, and love ourselves. We know that God is love, and we are taught that love conquers all. Yet why is it that we so seldom see love in our world? The evening news is but a litany of crimes and misdeeds, of deceit and violence. Our legal system operates to punish offenders; we have no comparable institution that rewards good! Our military complex defends us from potential intruders. Even our entertainment industry seems skewed toward depicting violence, crime, and all sorts of human degradation. Of course, these things have always existed, and perhaps they will always be with us. Such a constant bombardment of negativism makes us see the world as a place of fear rather than a place of opportunity, and life as filled with hatred rather than love. Unless we make a conscious, deliberate effort to seek love, we may fall into the trap of thinking that the world is inherently a bad place, a place where evil triumphs and where we must always be on our psychological guard. If we allow, the messages of the world would cut us off from our internal spiritual nurturing, rob us of our youthful spirit, and set the stage for accelerated aging, a brand of aging that brings anxiety rather than "good cheer."

## The Marble

The symbol for Key 2 is a marble. Why a marble? You may remember playing marbles when you were a kid, but I'd like you to think of something else for a moment. Think of the fact that approximately 6 billion people live on the face of this earth. Let's assume that each person on earth, each one of this 6 billion, does a hundred different things every day. These are everyday things such as getting up, brushing your teeth, saying hello to your neighbor, driving to the store. Each of these is considered one behavior. This means that 600 billion behaviors are performed each day. Now, think of each of these behaviors as a marble. Then imagine that standing in front of you is a mountain of these marbles, containing some 600 billion marbles. Personally, I cannot conceive of a pile of marbles that big, but try to do it anyhow. This huge pile of marbles is like a Mount Everest of marbles.

Now, imagine that every behavior you imagine to be "not good," morally speaking, is a red marble. Now also imagine that every behavior you consider to be morally upstanding—that is, which you imagine to be a behavior motivated by good—is a pink marble. So now you have, in your Mount Everest of marbles, some marbles that are red and some that are pink. Divide this one big mountain into two smaller piles of marbles, one red pile and one pink pile.

Now the question…*Which pile is bigger?* The red or the pink? The good or the not-good?

Your answer to this question becomes the fulcrum upon which swings the way you see the world. Do you live in a "red marble" world? Is your world basically a place of fear, a vale of tears, where there is weeping and gnashing of teeth, where most things that happen are wrong and out of line and chaotic? Is your world a bad place to live? Or do you live in a "pink marble" world? Does your world have order, principle, direction, understanding, and compassion? Is your world generally a good place to live?

It's amazing to me how many people will answer that certainly the red pile is much bigger than the pink pile. I'm always somewhat chagrined by such a response because as these people look out onto the world, they're not seeing love. They're seeing more hatred, evil, anger, trepidation, fear, discounting, and all manner of negative actions and motivations than they are seeing love. Evil is certainly resident in the world, but is it the true reality of the world?

We hear and read about evil all the time, don't we? The nightly news, for example, seems to be nothing more than an account of all that has gone wrong in our particular city, country, and world today. However, I don't think this is the balanced news; I believe that much more love occurs on this planet every day than there ever was evil. So why do we love so seldom? Why are our airwaves filled not with stories about love, but with stories about hate and fear, about what's wrong? Why do most of us seem to see only red marbles, without noticing very often all the pink marbles right next to them?

## Love and Fear

Dr. Gerald Jampolsky, M.D., author of *Love Is Letting Go of Fear,* asserts that *all* human action is either a statement of love or a request for love. This is a profound idea! What it tells us is that love is the premier motivating factor behind every human action; all human behavior is either a statement of love or a request for love.

It's easy to see how giving would be love, and even how receiving would be an act of love. We can understand how being a friend, or a parent, or even a workmate who cares are all roles primarily motivated by love. But we humans certainly find untold ways of *requesting* love in contorted ways. Can we see how a word said in a controlling or domineering manner could be a request for love? Can we see how an insult, or an intentional slight, or a meanspirited criticism could also be a request for love? Going further, what about a criminal, or a politician on the take, or an elder abuser: can we stretch our conceptions to see requests for love coming from these people? Our prisons are full of people who have asked for love in ways that our society does not sanction. We can all get very far afield in our behavior, losing our way in this world to such a degree that we seek love in ways that may be hurtful to other people. Some of us may have even done things that are unlawful. When we seek love in such self-serving ways, we are trying to aggrandize ourselves, trying to look better in the eyes of someone else. In the process, we are distorting love.

Our behavior, or that of others, may look like greed, may look like envy, may even look like jealousy, yet can we see it as a request for love? Can the need for love really underlie all these actions seeming to arise from hatred? It's hard for us to see everything like this, and I'm not suggesting that we can actually see love in every human action—that would be either superhuman or foolhardy. However, in my observations, those people who are most "youthful" and "ageless" are the same ones who seek to find love everywhere. At the very least, they find a basic positiveness in the human condition.

People who are spiritually mature try to seek love everywhere. When puzzled by someone else's behaviors, or by a condition in the world, they ask themselves the question *How could I see this differently?* They don't seem to jump to quick judgments about people, themselves, or their own behavior. Instead, they ask, *Where might there be a lesson of loving here?* They seem to believe simply that love is present in many, many forms, and that love is somewhere in this situation as well. They challenge themselves to look deeply into every situation and to observe even the simplest, smallest, most remote shard of love that might be there. Seek and you shall find.

I look in the morning paper and on the front page I see somebody who's in handcuffs being led into a squad car, having done some heinous thing to someone else. I could react negatively, my heart going out to the family or person who's the victim of this crime, and my heart hardening toward the accused perpetrator, certainly. But I could also ask, *Where is the love in this situation? Where can be the love?* and refuse to harden my heart toward the person who's committed the crime, because he's lost and needs love too.

Think of the worst possible thing that anyone could do. I think for me the example would be the Holocaust. How anyone could maliciously cause 6 million people to be slaughtered is beyond my comprehension. I ask myself, *How could I see this differently? How could I stop myself from being trapped into judging that the people who perpetrated this unbelievable crime are simply terrible?* As heinous as the Holocaust is, Christians are called, I believe, to search for the hand of God eventually manifesting itself in even this, the worst possible crime I and many people can imagine. Can we come to believe that the Holy Spirit will eventually create more good from this intolerable crime than the evil that ever came from it? This is faith; this is seeking for love.

Can our faith grow so strong as we mature into our senior-adult years that we can see love in situations in which the world sees only degradation, only dispute, or only evil? The people who have so grown in their faith, in ways both large and small, that they can seek God's love in all things, are the ones who seem to be radiant in spirit, regardless of their own situations or the condition of their own bodies.

## Aging Is Hastened by Fear

In *Love Is Letting Go of Fear,* Dr. Jampolsky also says that all emotions can be divided into two categories: love and fear. Fear confuses our thinking, represses our feelings, and distorts our true perception of ourselves and of others. Fear closes in on us. Being afraid is like walking into a darkened room and seeing only blackness. But when you fumble around and find the light string and pull it, the light goes on. Where does the darkness go? Who cares! It's gone! Light completely obliterates darkness. And love completely obliterates fear. Love clears our thinking, allows us full and honest expression of our feelings, and takes our blinders off so we can see accurately.

Isn't this the way of Jesus? When he taught, he didn't say, "Look how terrible this is over here" or "Don't do that." He used parables, saying, in essence, "Consider this person, consider this situation, consider this relationship." In effect, asking, "Where is the love here?" Jesus is the light that obliterates darkness, and when we see things through Jesus' point of view, we accurately see them in love.

Unfortunately, so much of what passes for teaching in our world today is not very much like the way Jesus taught. The world teaches by telling us what to avoid, rather than outlining the best way to go. I call this type of teaching "don't do this" and "don't do that" teaching. Another word for this is "fear" teaching.

Consider this: If I tell you, "Don't think of the letter Z," what do you immediately bring to mind? But if I say to you, "Would you think of the letter H," then you'll immediately bring to mind the letter H. The letter Z will be far from mind. That's the way Jesus taught. The stories he told show people how to live. He didn't curse the darkness, he turned on the light.

It's difficult to see and celebrate the light. Cursing the darkness is so much easier, because we're so accustomed to doing just that. But if we fill ourselves with negativity, we'll be unable to reach for the light string, and we'll be stuck in our darkness—and in our fear.

The more you fear, the more negative impulses, thoughts, feelings, and perceptions you are giving to your body. And the faster you are aging. Fear hastens aging. This is not simply a casual observation, but one I have gleaned from years and years of interacting with people in their senior years. Emerging medical research supports this observation.

The very popular physician-author Bernie Siegel, a renowned surgeon at Yale University who's written a number of books—*Love, Medicine, and Miracles; Peace, Love, and Healing;* and others—can teach us much about how our attitudes affect our aging. Dr. Siegel is an oncological surgeon. His professional life has revolved around taking out tumors, administering toxins called chemotherapy, and blasting people with potentially lethal waves called radiation therapy. But when Dr. Siegel reached mid-life and began an unwanted self-examination, he said to himself one day, "There must be a better way. I cannot keep mutilating people's bodies in the name of health. I need to perceive what I'm doing in a vastly different way. I could see this differently." Such ponderings started him on a magnificent journey that resulted in a new understanding of how the human organism works, as well as in his creating entirely new behavioral supplements for traditional cancer therapies.

Dr. Siegel tells us that when we see the world in what I would call a "pink marble" way, we're actually giving our body—giving the very cells that make up our body—messages that say, "Live in love." On the other hand, when we see the world in a "red marble" way, we're giving our bodies, at the cellular level, messages that say, "Live in fear." Through our own perceptions we give our bodies, at the most basic biological and chemical levels, messages of life and love, or messages of fear and death.

In other words, Dr. Siegel tells us, we can affect our own body chemistry. The way we see the world, and ourselves in it, determines the kind and level of chemicals our bodies produce. If we see the world as a good place where we can grow, be safe, and express ourselves, our bodies will produce chemicals that build, maintain, and care for us. If, on the other hand, we see the world as fearful, as a place where we must continuously protect ourselves, our bodies will deharmonize; eventually, this will erode and disorganize, weaken and exhaust us. When we approach the world with love as our primary purpose, we give "stay alive" messages to our internal pharmacy. When we see fear, guilt, and all manner of negative emotions, we give ourselves "die" messages that ultimately speed up our aging, making us simply "older" rather than ageless.

Not to downplay what modern science is learning, but we also have the teachings of Jesus to guide us in our reflections about fear. Jesus instructed us to fear not and to be of good cheer. Do you know the New Testament contains 365 references to this notion of "fear not"? I don't think that's a coincidence. Jesus is telling us—every single day— "Fear not, I am with you."

Being unafraid in the sense intended here means being willing to risk abandoning our preconceived notions—our dearly held judgments—in order to look beyond the world and see life through the eyes of Christ, through the eyes of love. "You are in this world but you are not of the world," Jesus told us, with the admonition to love everyone, even our enemies. Dr. Siegel took that risk when he embarked on his own spiritual journey because he was challenging the prevailing medical theories. Today he's a sought-after speaker, lecturer, and writer. He's also highly acclaimed as a potent reformer in the medical community. All of this resulted from his decision to see his career and his profession differently: to see it in love.

Love is everywhere because God, who is love, is everywhere. It is up to us to take the initiative and become aware of love—to focus on it. Love is the wellspring of vigor, the headwaters of freshness, and the waterfall of youthful spirit. Thriving people seek love in everything they do. Regardless of what appears in front of them on their path through life, they try to see it with love.

Christians are not called to live in some sort of Polyanna-ish way. We are not called to live with our heads in the clouds; we are to have our feet well planted on the ground, to be as realistic and as accurate as possible. And that means remembering this reality: that Christ came to us to exclaim the "Good News," and the good news is God *loves* us.

Love *really* is the primary motivational force of this world—indeed, of the universe. Love truly makes the world go 'round.

## Fountain of Youthfulness

Because people generally fear aging, they try to build up walls around it, or to prevent it. Many of us use anti-aging vitamins, anti-wrinkle cream, and an endless assortment of other concoctions to ward off aging or make us look younger. Ponce de Leon was not the only person who sought the fountain of youth. But if there is a fountain of youth, it's right inside of us. Our fountain of youthfulness springs from the way we perceive and think and feel and decide and act.

The fountain within us is a four-letter word starting with *L:* Love. Love is our fountain of youthfulness. When we seek love, when we seek to see love everywhere, when we tell ourselves we could see this or that differently, that "I could really see love if I wanted to," then we are giving ourselves "live and love" messages. We have found the fountain of youthfulness.

Dr. Siegel's work and other medical research point to the connection between our thoughts and emotions on the one hand and our physical and mental health on the other. No scientist or researcher in the world can say for sure why our bodies age. We simply know, proof positive, that they do. But the notion that we might somehow affect the pace of our aging is intriguing. Could it be that Christ's teachings of love are not only instructions for gaining eternal life but also directions for living a healthy physical and mental life right here as well?

## Aging As a Product of God's Love

We are all so like Saint Thomas, "doubting" Thomas, who had to see before he believed. But we must believe in love before we can see it. And that's what we are called to do.

Can we see aging as a product of God's love? Can we see the true maturation process as always asking us to become more youthful, and more youthful, and more youthful yet? The more you mature, the more you learn how to see love, and the more you are able to see love, the more youthful you will become. Youthfulness has nothing to do with your body. On the contrary, youthfulness has everything to do with how you can be "in love" by expressing your true, unique gifts. Youthfulness is that sparkling quality enabling your inner beauty to shine forth.

As we continue to see our own aging as a product of God's love, we will increasingly become more youthful in spirit. Regardless of our age, we will gradually move from pessimism to gratitude, from darkness to light, from criticism to care, and from pain to joy.

We will move from being fault-finders, which the world

would make of all of us, to love-finders, which Jesus would
have us be. The world advises us to seek fault. Jesus admonishes us to seek love.

As strange as it may seem, the world thinks that the bright-
est among us are the ones who can find the most fault. According to the world, your job today and every day is to go
out there and find out what's wrong. Is that what you really
want to do every day—find out what's wrong with everything? If you want to age fast, go find out what's wrong
with the world and everyone in it. Complain about everything. See the negative side of everything.

On the other hand, if you want to grow into youthfulness, find love everywhere. Say to yourself, "I could see
love here. There is love here. It's my job to find it." Now
you're living in a totally different world, are you not?

Do you want to live in a fault-finding world, or do you
want to live in a love-finding world? It's really a simple
question to answer.

## How to Seek Love Everywhere

Jesus asks us to seek love. But how are we to seek love
everywhere? And what is *love* anyway? *Love* is a huge concept. How can we possibly define it? In my book *Body,
Mind, Spirit* I tried, but it was a most feeble attempt. I'm
afraid that I diminished Love tremendously.

I think that the best way to seek love is to look for virtue.
We can see love in the world because we can observe virtue. I define *virtue* as "love in action." Think of any virtue:
hope, mercy, faith, perseverance, acceptance, stamina,
simplicity...the list goes on. Each of these is a different
way of acting in love, of being love. If we can train our

perception to become aware of virtue, then we will see love…what love is on this plane.

And we can take decisive steps to find God's love. Each morning as we arise, we can spend time in prayer, asking for God's guidance. We can fill our minds with love, learning to find it in everyone we meet and in everything we do. We can, from time to time, vacate this world and go to God who holds the lamp that illuminates our true selves. Throughout the day we can find ourselves meditating on the seeming paradox that our aging is actually challenging us and providing us with opportunities to mature in faith and spirit, and in so doing, to become youthful and ageless.

Throughout the day take mini-love vacations. Take thirty seconds, close your eyes, and ask yourself, "Where can I see love in the next five minutes?" Walking down a hallway, imagine that love is behind every door. Let yourself find it. Because if we believe the opposite, then what would we be looking for? "Seek and you shall find. Knock and it will be opened to you." If you seek fear, you'll find it. If you seek love, you'll find it. This is the wisdom that comes with aging. Be not afraid to seek love everywhere, for if you do, you will certainly find the fountain of youthfulness.

# Key 3

---

# Delight in Connectedness

*If we say that we have fellowship with him while we are walking in darkness, we lie and do not do what is true; but if we walk in the light as he himself is in the light, we have fellowship with one another.*

1 John 1:6–7

**Key 3 Definition:** The degree to which we can deeply share ourselves with others and find joy therein.

## Connectedness:
## The Core of Our Earthly Journey

**Y**outhfulness, or what we are also calling agelessness, the quality of living in a vital and vibrant manner, is much more a product of one's beliefs than it is a measure of one's age. Indeed, it has very little if anything to do with age. Youthfulness does *not* mean acting as though you were young. You'll never be young again (thank goodness!), but as you mature, you can become increasingly more youthful. One must be very mature in order to become ever more youthful. Spiritual youthfulness comes more from one's awakening attitudes and values than from one's resumé of accomplishments and experiences.

A number of factors characterize youthfulness, among which is one's ability to connect and interact in meaningful ways with one's neighbors…God's children. Let's explore the meaning of connectedness, the third key to spiritual vitality.

So many times my clients will ask, "Will I become so self-absorbed like my aging parent? All she (he) wants to do is talk about herself (himself)." I always answer with the same response, "Not if you remain interested in the lives and welfare of others! Not if you grow into youthfulness." The question behind the question is this: *Is it inevitable that I become self-absorbed and self-centered in my senior years?* The answer is a resounding "No!" Your age has nothing to do with your interest level in others. Some younger people, however, have the impression that senior adults simply lose their desire, or perhaps their ability, to remain empathetically interested in the lives of others…even their own family. This myth is so prevalent that our culture has come to believe that self-centeredness is associated with aging, while empathy, the ability to relate deeply with another, is associated with youthfulness.

Christians are called to connectedness. Christ's central message of love hinges on empathy. Our ability to relate or "connect" with others is at the core of what we are supposed to learn here on our earthly journey. We cannot show the love we have for God to God alone. We must, in our own ways, find connections with other people, with all God's children. Here, then, is the secret of maintaining a youthful spirit as we mature, of recognizing our emerging agelessness.

## We Connected Well As Children

As children, we seemed to be able to connect very well with others. We entered into play and enjoyed many kinds of experiences and relationships with other children, whether it was in parallel play, or inclusive play, or any other kind of play. We shared ourselves and showed concern and even compassion for others, including adults. We freely related and shared ideas, suggestions, and laughter. We know this was true for most of us because we can observe now how easily children enjoy one another, how easy and genuine it seems for them.

As we have matured, however, somehow some of us have lost our abilities for connecting with others. Certainly, we can all point to phases in our lives when we seemed to relate more smoothly than at other times, but generally our personalities have remained rather consistent over the years. Yet as we enter into the senior stages of growth, we may tend to magnify certain of our personality traits, perhaps as a result of the inevitable losses we have experienced in moving along the life span. Some of us may experience the unhealthy tendency to drift toward isolation, to shift our thinking toward excluding rather than including.

For many elders, this slight drift away from interpersonal connectedness, this drift toward isolation, can breed despondency. In extreme cases, this isolation can become reclusiveness. Reclusiveness brings on aloneness, and aloneness makes us lonely. Loneliness and depression are the co-conspirators of many maladies of the body, mind, and spirit in one's senior years.

A model that can help us understand the relationship between sickness and the lack of connectedness is what I call the *Three Ss Model.* The first *S* stands for *stress,* the second for *strain,* and the third for *sickness.*

All of us feel stress, which is simply a consequence of living in this modern world. Stress can come from things that we would consider normal, like meeting a deadline at work or organizing a birthday party. There's also stress that comes from things that we would rather not be normal, like traffic jams or doctor's bills.

Some stress is actually good. We call this type of stress "eustress." The prefix *eu* is the same one that begins the word *euphoria,* meaning "of good spirits." So eustress is good stress. When you got out of bed this morning, it was eustress that helped you do it. If you didn't experience the eustress that "pushed" you out of bed, you wouldn't ever be able to interact with others. However, getting caught in that traffic jam on the freeway this morning was probably not eustressful; on the contrary, it was probably distressful. Distress is the opposite side of the stress coin from eustress.

When left unabated to continue and increase, distress becomes the second *S* in our model—*strain.* Strain means that something in your bodily organic system is being stretched, and tested, and pushed, perhaps even to a potential breaking point. For example, the distressful daily traffic jam can become a real strain because of its relentlessness, and if you have a particularly important appointment one day, you could feel as if you're being strained to a breaking point.

This leads us to the third *S* in our model—*sickness.* When left unabated, stress produces strain; and strain, when left unintervened upon, becomes sickness. For example, if it continues long enough, the strain of battling the daily traffic to get to important meetings on time could eventually make you very sick.

Many studies have looked at how we can stop this stress-strain-sickness cycle, and much has been discovered. One such study is reported in the book *The Hardy Executive* by Salvatore Maddi and Suzanne Kobasa. The first thing that these researchers found was that we can help prevent strain from degenerating into sickness by injecting health practices into the very fabric of our lives. Health practices would include eating properly, exercising adequately, getting sufficient sleep, and moderating our intake of alcohol, as well as inducing relaxation by meditating, praying, listening to good music, and the like. These kinds of things allow us to reduce some of the organic or biological consequences of the strain that comes from normal living. Health practices work very well in preventing strain from becoming sickness.

You might think that senior adults don't have the same stress that they had in their earlier years. This may be true, but consider this: We normally think of stress as coming from situations that overtax us, when we have too much stimulation bombarding us from all sides and we just can't cope with it all. Researchers have found that stress can come from exactly the opposite as well. We can experience stress when we are not receiving *enough* stimulation. We can actually increase our stress when we deprive ourselves of activity, when we decline to become engaged in projects, when we shy away from participating in potentially enjoyable ventures with others. So we can experience stress on both ends of the spectrum: stress from both too much stimulation and too little!

But what can we do about stress? Are there ways we can prevent our culturally endemic stress from becoming strain? The answer is yes, and Maddi and Kobasa have identified four characteristics that seem to prevent stress from growing into strain. All four of these characteristics begin with the letter *C*.

The first *C* is *challenge*. Adults who can look at the world as a challenging place, not as a threatening place, seem much healthier.

The second *C* is *control*. Adults who exercise control don't feel helpless in this world; they feel as if they can influence events by themselves. They have some level of control.

The third *C* stands for *committed*. Committed adults don't feel alienated from the world; instead, they feel committed to some goal, quest, mission, or ministry. They are actively pursuing something.

The fourth *C*, you have probably already guessed, stands for *connectedness*. When a person is connected, it means that they are "in the loop" of life; they are involved in the active stream of energy that is love. When a person can relate to other people at an intimate—that is, in a sharing—kind of way, that person is giving her or himself a unique gift, the gifts of a loving life. Disconnectedness, however, sets us up for discouragement and disappointment. When we become separated for an extended period, we eventually become sick physically, mentally, or spiritually. We feel disconnected, uninvolved, alienated; these are all potent risk factors for disease of some sort.

In a landmark study that researched the personal effectiveness of managers and supervisors, it was discovered that "connectedness," the ability to relate constructively with others, is a critical means of handling stress. It's long been recognized that some persons can thrive under the same stressful conditions that cause others to collapse emotionally. Why? There must be something that protects those who thrive from the otherwise damaging effects of stress overload. Researchers found once again that a person's decisions to share themselves with others, their choice to relate to and enjoy others, enabled them not only to withstand stress, but to thrive in it.

## Slight Drift toward Isolation

I once gave an address to a large gerontology conference. As I raised my voice to a crescendo, I asked the whole group, "What is it that older people are really interested in?" I intended the question to be simply rhetorical. However, this little elder woman who was sitting right in front of my podium yelled out, "Their bowels!"

I think this is rather descriptive of what happens when a person becomes increasingly disconnected. When they become disconnected from other people, they easily become more and more interested in themselves. They become self-absorbed.

Senior adults who fall into such an emotional posture are quite unaware they are doing so. Yet it's more than noticeable to those around them. Adult children seem particularly disturbed by their aging parent's increasing self-concern. "She used to be so interested in my life and my family. We would visit together often and enjoy quality time. Now she seems concerned only with herself." Laments like this one are unfortunately common among adult children with aging parents.

This self-absorption many times manifests as obsessive interest in their own body. Daily bodily functions become very important for some older persons, as do all their medical needs and doctor's appointments. And when we ask an older person the question we should never ask them—that is, *How are you today?*—we get the "organ recital," a regular litany of all the aches and pains they are feeling bodily. (A bit of advice—and I mean this in a most sincere and authentic way: don't ask an older person how they are. Do not ask, "How are you today?" The question is interpreted on a physical level only and generally focuses the resultant conversation onto medical topics, which can be awfully boring and impersonal, rather than on the much more profitable issues of personal interest and care. Much better to say to them, "Good to see you today, Frances"; "Good to see you today, Bill.")

This increasing interest in the physical self shows the drift away from connectedness. Study after study of what brings life satisfaction—a full measure of happiness experienced in one's senior years—arrives at the same conclusion: the presence of a confidant, the presence of a person with whom you share your life, your fears, your joys, your sorrows, your everything, exerts a tremendously positive and health-enhancing impact upon adults! The presence of a confidant seems to go a long way toward providing that balance between only surviving and really thriving. If you have a confidant, take very good care of this person, because when you look in their eyes what you're seeing is a good measure of your mental wellness. If you don't have a confidant...go get one!

## Connectedness Includes...

People have said to me, "What am I supposed to communicate with other people? How do I connect with another person?" First, we need to understand that by connectedness I mean the capacity to communicate our feelings fully. But what are our feelings? Our feelings are everything that is going on within us—our fears and worries and concerns, certainly, but also our hopes and happinesses and dreams. Second, by connectedness I also mean the capacity to be warmly understanding of other people's feelings. To be warmly understanding means to solicit the deep feelings of other people. We call that being empathic. Third, connectedness means the ability to compliment another. This means putting aside our own agendas in order to let someone know that they have done a wonderful thing. Fourth, to generate connectedness, we must make ourselves available to meet other people's needs, and to do so we must get to know the other well enough to discern what is truly in their best interest. Overall, connectedness means communicating an eagerness to "be with" someone else, the desire to really want to know them where they are.

I've done lots and lots of work with the adult children of aging parents. Time after time I am struck by the similarity of their stories, particularly those of adult children who are daughters. The story many of these women relate goes something like this:

"You know, my mother used to be a good friend. I really looked forward to going out to lunch with her or to spending some time with her. She's was interested in me, and I was interested in her, and we could share. She was interested in what I was doing in my life, my kids, my relationships, my faith, and so on—things that were going on in my life. She would ask me questions, and I could share. She would be happy for me when I was happy, and she could share my sadness when those low times came. We shared together.

"Now, something has changed. I've noticed in recent years that I don't look forward to going out to lunch with her like I used to. I seem to be cutting her short, cutting down on the amount of time I spend with her. When I ask myself why, what I come up with is so unfortunate, such a loss for us both. She seems interested only in herself. She seems to concentrate almost exclusively on her medical issues. She wants to tell me about what she had for breakfast, or how the delivery man was late, or how terrible her arthritis is getting. It's not that I'm disinterested in her physical or emotional well-being, or even what she eats, but our conversations and her interests seem so one-sided, so self-centered. It feels like I've lost a confidante."

This shift I've noticed, especially in the mother-daughter relationship, is a very large developmental disappointment for adult children. This story strikes me as a good summation of one of the unhealthy consequences of self-absorption, and a good indication that those people who can remain emotionally connected—that is, remain interested in other people—mature the best and develop most healthfully.

At its center, connectedness means remaining interested in other people. Connectedness also includes appreciation, gratefulness, and love. The only place you can find love is in other people. This, of course, builds on the Key 2, "Seek Love Everywhere." Part of connectedness is the ability to be grateful; to have appreciation for the wonderful gifts God has given us.

Another characteristic of healthy adults who connect with others is their ability to give compliments. We're not talking about something that's ungenuine, like flattery. We're talking about searching the horizon for ways that we can sincerely tell another person, "Hey, you're doing great." Even if all you can think of is "I like the shirt you're wearing today." That's wonderful! At least we're focusing on the other person, because the simple fact is that focusing on ourself exclusively is detrimental to our health.

Finally, connectedness includes expressing love through understanding what another person's needs are and actually doing something meaningful for that person. This does not mean that we do everything for them, because that would lead to infantilization. We infantilize another person when we "take over" their lives, doing so much for them that they don't even have to think for themselves. Of course, we don't want to do this with anyone.

Seeking things that are really beneficial for another person sometimes means that we must say "no." Have you ever noticed how difficult it is to say "no" to your mother or father, and by extension to older people in general? Did you ever ask yourself why that is so?

Shirley was this way, never able to say "no" to her mother. Shirley's mother liked to watch a particular "soap" on TV. Unfortunately, the time of the show was changed to the very half-hour when her mother liked to take her nap. Instead of changing her nap time, Shirley's mother asked if Shirley could tape the show and bring it over each night. Unbelievably, Shirley couldn't say "no"; and as far as I know, she is still taping the show and dutifully taking it over to her mom's each evening.

I believe that in each of us is a three-year-old child. What that three-year-old child wants more than anything else is love. A three-year-old is a love-seeking machine. When you were three years old, you knew there were giants walking around your house. You called them parents. In your eyes they knew everything and provided you with unending love. The worst thing that could possibly happen to you was for one of your parents to withdraw their love from you. In your three-year-old mind, losing the love of your parents was the worst possible tragedy you could imagine. So you did everything you could to please them.

One of the things you didn't say with real meaning to your parents was "no." Even though you may have in the tempestuous twos had temper tantrums during which you liberally used the word *no,* when it really came down to it, you never really wanted to displease your mother or your father.

As we mature, this tendency doesn't go away; indeed, it seems to increase in strength as we get older. We seem to have some deeply held belief that says we will somehow self-destruct if we don't do everything we can for our parents. Make no mistake about it, your little love-seeking three-year-old self is still within you today, no matter how old you are. We are all love-seeking machines, whether we're thirteen or twenty-three or thirty-three or eighty-three.

Of course, we in the Judeo-Christian tradition have the guidance of the Fourth Commandment, "Honor thy father and thy mother." For me, as I suspect for others as well, the Fourth Commandment was the first commandment I was taught. And we may not have been taught, or may not remember, that there is more to it than "Honor thy father and thy mother." The Fourth Commandment is the only one of the ten that gives us a promise. What is that promise? "And your days will be long upon this land." How true we are finding this to be!

What does the word *honor* mean in the Fourth Commandment? We think it means "respect." Some people even say it means "obey." The actual translation of the word *honor* is "do not abandon." In this sense, this commandment becomes a difficult burden for some adult children. Some people think, for example, that they are abandoning Mom when it becomes necessary for her to move to a skilled nursing facility. Not true! Honoring your parents means that you do what you can to ensure their safety, their care, and their needs. Many times, the only place where all this can happen is in a nursing facility. In a very real sense, honoring them means loving them and caring for them in the best way possible, not abandoning them to muddle along as best they can. (Interestingly enough, you are not called to like them.)

This final aspect of connectedness, one's willingness to offer something of oneself to others, adds measurably to youthfulness. It is the opposite of self-centeredness, and we commonly call it altruism. Altruism is giving of yourself without expecting any compensation in return. Over the years, psychology has had a difficult time explaining altruism and has even denied its very existence. Yet too many people are doing too many things for which they want or expect nothing in return, for altruism to be ignored further.

Volunteering is perhaps the classic altruistic act and perhaps the highest level of connectedness that we can achieve. Expecting nothing for ourselves, we give ourselves freely to others, sometimes other people we don't even know. Volunteering is practicing connectedness in a way that says, "I care about you...I want the best for you!" Altruism is a pure act of love, an extension of God's central message to God's children.

Recently, we've discovered that people who volunteer

exhibit overall wellness in ways far beyond those of persons who do not volunteer. Once again, we see that enjoyable interaction with others not only connects us with God and encourages our spiritual development but generates youthfulness as well.

In years past I taught graduate medical residents the "art" rather than the science of practicing medicine. I would tell the medical residents that if they were really serious about helping people to be as well as possible, and if they really wanted to be truly beneficial to their patients in a holistic manner, they must encourage them to connect with other people. This is just as important as any instructions about proper diet, sleeping habits, moderation of alcohol use, and proper exercise.

## Profound Buffer against Alienation

Connectedness is a profound buffer against alienation. Sharing on an intimate level creates for us a life-invigorating energy and happiness that we can achieve in no other way. Could it be then that Christ's admonition to love our neighbor is not only a vehicle for spiritual development but is also a means of maintaining wellness? Could it be that Christ's teaching is really a profound way of saying what psychology has only recently learned, that our ability to make and keep friends is a premier benchmark of our overall wellness? Pursuing intimacy seems to fortify us to be ever more emotionally healthy. Enjoying other people's company, it would seem, is life enhancing from almost every perspective.

## The Daisy

The symbol for this third key is a daisy. A daisy is a beautiful flower that exemplifies a simple yet profound love. The petals of a daisy are connected to the central portion, or eye, of the daisy. In addition, all the petals are interconnected; the petals overlap, and in so doing form a perfect circle of connectedness. We are to be no less here on this earth. We are to form perfect circles of love through our interconnections with others. We are the petals of the daisy of love, and in connecting with others we find our ultimate connectedness with God.

# Key 4

---

# Live in the Now

*For I am convinced that neither death, nor life, nor angels, nor rulers, nor things present, nor things to come, nor powers, nor height, nor depth, nor anything else in all creation, will be able to separate us from the love of God in Christ Jesus our Lord.*

Romans 8:38–39

**Key 4 Definition:** The degree to which we are aware of and can focus on our present reality.

The symbol for living in the now is an orange. Why an orange? Think about the purpose of eating an orange. To get our daily dose of vitamin C? To get enough fiber? Perhaps simply to enjoy the wonderful taste?

Let's use the orange to illustrate how we can live in the now. There are two ways of eating an orange. One way is to get the orange from outside of you down into your stomach in the most efficient way possible. This we could call the utilitarian way of eating an orange.

Another way of eating an orange we might call the sensational way. First, take the orange in your hands and fondle it. Appreciate its texture, its color, and its packaging. All the promotional know-how of all the advertising agencies on Madison Avenue could never put together packaging like this. Notice all the little dimples on the orange and how it's so wonderfully molded and shaped. Dig your thumbs into the skin of the orange and experience the vapor, the essence of the citrus, as it escapes from the orange peel. Gradually unwrap the orange until all of the peel is off and the orange is clean. Feel the smooth "meat" of the orange. Appreciate its wonderful sensation.

Break open the orange where the wedges divide, and separate out a wedge. Appreciate this marvelous bite-size piece of wonder. Now pop the wedge into your mouth and play with it. Feel the coolness and the softness of the wedge, how smooth and supple it is. Now put the orange wedge between your teeth, squeeze, and feel that explosion of flavor and freshness and coolness; be grateful for the refreshment that comes from this sensation. Then chew it up and feel that nutritious substance go down into your stomach.

It's clear that this second way of eating an orange, unlike the first, allows us to savor the fruit, experiencing it fully and appreciating the true reality of the orange.

Life is like eating an orange. It can be utilitarian, or it can be sensational. Many of us, unfortunately, eat the orange of life at the same time we're doing sixteen other things. We're reading the newspaper or driving the car and worrying about where we're going or watching television. We're thinking about a thousand different things and not fully focusing on the truth, beauty, and goodness that is in front of us right now. While we're eating the orange we're thinking about what tomorrow will bring, what we're going to do the next hour, tonight, tomorrow, next week, next month. We're always wondering about other things, and we're missing the genuine reality of the moment that is unfolding right in front of us.

## Spiritual Vitality Means Living in the Present

The popular author and psychologist Wayne Dyer says simply, "Yesterday is a canceled check, tomorrow is promised to no one, the only thing you have is right now." Right now is passing at such a fast pace that we don't have it for very long. The "right now" of a few seconds ago is gone forever; what did we do with it?

When is the only time we can love? When is the only time we can live? We can't live or love yesterday, we can't live or love tomorrow. The only time we have is right now, and our only goal today is to learn how to love better. The only way you can learn how to love better is to experience love now. Right here in the present.

It takes great energy for us to focus like a laser beam exclusively on this present moment of life, this piece of our earthly existence, this wonderful gift. This *Augenblick,* this blink of an eye, as the Germans would say, moves so quickly from us. Our life is really a succession of present moments.

## Past Thinking Breeds Guilt, Future Thinking Breeds Fear

Many times, however, our mind is preoccupied with so many thousands of other things. Mentally, we find ourselves living either in the future or in the past. We miss what's happening right now.

When we focus on the past, we feel either pleasure or pain. Sometimes we can reminiscence and feel good about the past, enjoying our memories and their associations. But we often feel a sense of regret. We may internally say to ourselves, "I should have done something other than what I did" or "Why didn't I do something else? I could have. I should have." In a sense, we are constantly judging ourselves. We play the "should" game: "I should have been more...I shouldn't have been so...I should have bought Coca-Cola stock back in 1958...I should never have bought this car...." We constantly "should" all over ourselves. The inevitable consequence of the "should" game is guilt. So many of us feel such guilt.

We are all products of our past to a greater or lesser degree, yet we are not prisoners of it. Living in the present requires that we make the choice to live today, to enter into a fuller mindfulness of the moment. Anthony de Mello, S.J., the noted Jesuit author and speaker, devoted his entire ministerial life to one simple yet profound idea, preaching over and over again the importance of awareness. "Wake up," he would say. All of his talks, retreats, stories, seminars, and books echoed the same theme: wake up, become aware of the love that is all around you. Mindfulness, awakening, full awareness all depend upon our living in the now.

When we project into the future, we can encounter other unhealthy and youth-robbing emotions, most notably those associated with fear. Fear is the emotional result of imposing the past upon the future. Internally, we give ourselves the message *It happened before, so it will surely happen again.* The event that we remember, and hence fear will reoccur, is the one we have already judged as being destructive to us in the past. Therefore, we "predict" the future based upon the worst of what has happened previously.

The assumption that we unwittingly make is that past is destined to repeat itself over and over again. We assume that today will be just like yesterday, and that tomorrow will be the same as today. Logically, this would mean that we could never grow. And indeed, we seem to fear that we will never grow, that we can never change.

One of the ways that we deal with this fear is to project it onto another person. We don't like feeling fear, so we give it to someone else. *Projection* means that we mentally push our own fear out onto those around us. In such a way we attempt to live within a blissful illusion that we're not fearful but that everything outside of us is fearful. Eventually, we "decide" that this world is a fearful place because wherever we place our gaze we find fear instead of love. If we do this over and over and over, every place we look in this world becomes fearful, something to be on guard against. Gradually, all the "nows" of our life become simply preparations for future security.

One thing almost everyone fears is pain. Trying to avoid pain is natural, but when the fear of possible future pain prevents us from living in the present, it's a problem. Even the thought of possible future pain can ruin our day.

Our world has become masterfully adept at taking advantage of our fear of pain, at motivating us with fear. This is particularly true when it comes to our body. Have you ever had an experience like the following? You're driving down the street, enjoying the beautiful day. The birds are chirping, the tulips are blooming, and you're thinking beautiful thoughts. You flip on the radio to hear some nice music, then along comes a "health information bulletin" from

St. Somebody Hospital: "Are you sure your pancreas is OK? Your pancreas may be causing problems for your whole body. You never know when something bad is happening. Pancreatic disease is on an upswing, you know. Perhaps you should have your pancreas checked out. St. Somebody has a new Pancreas Assessment Unit. Call to make an appointment right now." So you start thinking to yourself, *Pancreas? Where is my pancreas? Could my pancreas be malfunctioning? I better get over to St. Somebody's and have my pancreas checked out!*

You have let your beautiful day slip right away, for your thoughts are now only of the past—*Something must have happened to my pancreas*—or of the future—*I need to get over to St. Somebody Hospital right away.* And instead of being happy, you are now miserable. Why let your pancreas, or anything, cloud over the love you can experience in the present moment?

We will all experience pain, but the thought of it need not terrify us. I remember talking to a female physician who once said an interesting thing. "You know," she commented, "one thing I think people have to realize is that living is painful. We all get aches and pains from living. These are normal, natural things that happen in a person's life. It doesn't mean that something's wrong every time we have a pain. We don't have to go to the doctor every time we have some sort of pain. Pain is a natural part of living, and you will get over it."

Many times we are caught in a mental vice, squeezed between the guilty past on the one side and the fearful future on the other. And the squeezing leaves very little room for us to experience life fully in the now. So we choose to live in a state of yesterday or tomorrow and never truly "own" our todays, which become either leftovers from yesterday or prefaces for tomorrow.

## Today's Reality Is Love

Today's reality is the reality of love. Jesus, as you know, brought a new way, the good news of love. To love as Jesus taught, we must focus on the present. We need to see time differently. We need to realize that even though we have a past and a hopeful, Christ-centered future, our main sight is on the eternal Now. Today is a fully unique time, a time for love in a special way, a time for redemption. The past, the present, and the future are one continuous extension of a unifying whole, which we can call the mind of God in the love of Christ.

When we think in these terms, we align ourselves with Jesus' message of love. Whatever has become and will become after Christ can never be the same as what came before. Likewise, as we more completely accept Christ in our most intimate selves, we realize that both past and future are meaningful only as they reflect upon today. Christ can only operate in the present. Our true self, that self which is of God, exists not yesterday, not tomorrow, but only today. Our loving God is "I AM," never "I was" or "I will be."

## Reminiscing in the Now

Reminiscing has long been misunderstood as the idle wanderings of a diminishing mind that has nothing better to do than look back to a more meaningful time of life. There is no question that reminiscing is "looking to the past," and in some forms it can be unhealthy. Reminiscing, however, can be very present-focused and life-giving. When it is, reminiscing can be a powerful youthfulness enhancer for you.

Our perceptions of the past determine what kind of internal messages we give ourselves today. Messages of love and life produce youthfulness, while messages of fear and death bring accelerated aging. If your reminiscing is simply wishing that today were more like yesterday, then it will produce only negative emotions. On the other hand, if your reminiscing helps you accept God's grace and feel God's love in the present, then you can look at your life thus far and say, "I can see God's invisible hand in all that I've experienced in my life, both the 'good' and the 'bad.'" When this is your response, then peace, love, hope, and trust will be your youth-giving reward.

Reminiscing, or *life review,* is now recognized as a practice that is almost universal among senior adults. Life review is *not* the idle wandering of an unfocused mind, as some people see it. It is a powerful therapeutic modality for mental health, as well as a potent way of dealing with middle- and later-life depression.

What is life review, really? Literally, it means "to see one's life again." Life review is looking at a piece of your past life and recognizing that there was something good, wholesome, and constructive about a particular event. Ultimately, what happens in life review is the realization, on a spiritual level, that God's hand has always been on your life. The marvelous consequence for a Christian is the profound understanding that what has happened in one's life has happened by design; some plan is being played out. Not that God was dictating or predestining our lives, but that in some way we were in communion or connected with the eternal presence of God all through our lives.

This realization helps us to understand that God has no past, present, or future. God is the ultimate eternal present. And our mission is to connect with the person and presence of God in the eternal Now.

## Integrity versus Despair

Eric Erickson, regarded as the premier adult developmentalist of our time, calls the last stage of living "integrity versus despair." Integrity means having wholeness. The ultimate extension of wholeness is holiness. The opposite of holiness and wholeness is fragmentation or despair: when we feel as if we're in pieces.

People in their later years can manifest two forms of despair. One we euphemistically call "cantankerousness." This is the angry person, someone who is usually critical, dogmatic, inflexible, and, on the surface at least, absolutely sure of what she/he is saying. Angry persons are usually frightening. An angry older person is basically saying that his life has not been good, and that you're to blame. This person has not been able to build integrity into his life. He has somehow lost sight of any unifying principles. He looks at his life and says, "What for? It wasn't good. Something's been flawed about this."

I remember Harry, a resident in a senior housing building in a small southern city. I visited Harry several times at the request of the housing director who was worried about him. He presented a pathetic picture. His small efficiency apartment was stark: no pictures, only a chair, couch, table, and bed. At first I thought he suffered from Alzheimer's since he appeared so dissolved. His demeanor was guarded and his eyes seemed frightened, but from the moment he uttered his first words to me I could feel his stiff veneer was more like an armor he wore to keep out the world. He was angry; indeed, he seemed unable to project anything but bitterness. After three visits, my efforts to "reach" him were not received as acts of compassion but rather as rude intrusions into his anger-protected inner life. I never saw Harry again. I do remember him, though, as a broken man, who had adopted an offensive personality of cantankerousness.

The second kind of despair is self-hatred. Like the angry person, the self-hater or the depressed personality will lament that his or her life has not been good. The big difference is that instead of blaming others for their internal torture, depressed persons blame themselves; they claim that all their problems are their own fault. Basically, they are telling themselves, "I don't have any integrity, I don't have connectedness. I'm unable to live in the now."

Denise, age eighty-three and meticulously groomed, entered my office with the grace of a model walking down a fashion show runway. She had been referred to me by her physician, who felt Denise had slipped into depression. While her words were social, they were also sparse and clipped; they hung in the air like dewdrops about to fall to the ground. With great difficulty, she explained to me how she had lost so much in these last years. Yet what she related were not items of great import. She had lost her husband some twenty years earlier, and this major loss was conspicuously absent from her litany. What she did relate were losses that all related to her own person: her ability to walk, think, sleep, prepare food, and even see. When I asked if she had friends, she said that she had lost most of them because she couldn't write anymore. I inquired what she meant, and she insisted that she simply couldn't write. I asked her to copy a sentence in her own handwriting. She quickly copied it in quite legible script. When I remarked that she certainly could write, she quipped, "Not like I used to." Evidently, she was proud of her formerly perfect Palmer-method handwriting, which she could no longer duplicate. Denise *was* depressed, but neither her handwriting nor her other losses had robbed her of her friends…her unfortunate depression had. She couldn't stop protesting how inadequate she had become.

Erickson would say that through life review we are building integrity today, the opposite of despair. Both Harry and Denise would be well served by life review. Looking back at one's life, and "making sense of it," is not the same as living in the past, even though we're thinking about the past. It's a present-focused activity. In life review we identify the principles and the underpinnings that create the wholeness of our lives. We come to recognize ever more clearly that our life is whole, and therefore holy.

## Understanding Our Own Needs

In the last chapter, we learned what it means to "be with" another person, and how that differs from "doing for" someone. It's a hard lesson to incorporate into one's life, and so many times I see adult-children caregivers not "being with" their elder parents but trying to "do for" them. When the accent of a relationship is constantly on "doing for" them, rather than emotionally, psychologically, and spiritually "being with" them, the ultimate result is a burned-out caregiver.

One of the things that hurts me so is to see a good caregiver—a person who is devoting a good portion of his life, professionally, personally, or both, to the care of an elder person in need—"bite the dust." By this I mean that internal and external factors so push her that she collapses. It's not that she doesn't care; on the contrary, it may be that she cares too much, or that she cares in ways that are unhealthy for her and her aging parent. She gives, gives, gives, emotionally depleting herself. What does she do with her last ounce of energy? She gives it away. She has nothing left. She is simply burned out.

Denise's daughter is a good example. Joyce was the consummate dutiful daughter. She devoted a good part of her day to thinking about and "doing for" her mother. Denise's advancing depression placed more and more strain upon Joyce. "How can I help my mother?...What can I do for her to snap her out of the 'funk' she's fallen into?" As Joyce focused more and more of her energies onto her mom, she had less and less energy to take care of herself. Ultimately, Joyce "crashed": she too became depressed and found scant joy in her life. She had succumbed to the strain of caring for an aging parent and had "bitten the dust."

Have you ever been burned out? I certainly have. Burnout has many consequences. It can make us feel depressed. We can seem unable to have fun. We can feel a sense of hopelessness and uselessness. We can feel guilty. Ultimately, burnout will manifest itself physically: we simply get sick.

Having done several research studies on caregivers, I have found that their morbidity (sickness) level is statistically higher than that of the rest of the population because they give themselves away too much. When we push too hard for too long, the consequence is generally some sort of sickness, whether emotional, physical, or even spiritual. We must maintain the balance between giving of ourselves and taking care of ourselves. To do so, we must recognize our own needs and act on them, rather than acting solely on behalf of others. Balancing our own and others' needs is part of learning how to live in the now.

If we find ourselves burned out, we need to begin making some difficult choices. Some sort of life modification would be appropriate: time off, a change of pace, the introduction of a new prayer life, perhaps some counseling. We need to get off the assembly line, as it were, for awhile. Burnout does not get better if ignored.

Faced with choices that might seem selfish and alternatives that might seem agonizing, a caregiver might find herself paralyzed by indecision. In such circumstances, it is important to realize that people make important, life-altering choices every moment of their life. Most of the time they are blissfully unaware that they are even making these choices. Here are seventeen such choices that we're making every "now" moment. How "awake" are you to each of these decisions? You have the power—indeed, you have the mandate—at every moment of your life to choose between

- the Holy Spirit or the world
- wakefulness or sleep
- forgiveness or condemnation
- love finding or fault finding
- peace or turmoil
- the light of Christ or the darkness of the world
- freedom or confinement
- unity or separation
- heaven or hell
- joy and well-being or fear
- meaning or meaninglessness

- truth or error
- vision or blindness
- being happy or being right
- learning or existing
- being of value or being worthless
- living internally or living externally

How mindful are any of us to these present-moment choices? Most times it's much easier to sleepwalk through life, as Father de Mello would say. We simply go through the motions of the day, performing our tasks, busying ourselves with this and that. We are only minimally aware of the tremendous panorama of choice we have. Just as the simple act of eating an orange has so much beauty that we generally overlook, God's children, ourselves included, possess a vast beauty that we simply choose to ignore. We simply aren't awake to it because we're so busy living in the past or in the future. Even on a mundane level, when we live in the past or in the future, we have difficulty experiencing any fun. This lesson is not just for caregivers. There will be no joy in Mudville, not for any of us, if we don't live to some degree in the now.

In his book *Elder Wisdom,* Eugene Bianchi describes how he assembled a number of elders who were, by all accounts and measures, living highly fulfilling and enjoyable lives. His research sought to identify those factors that gave this group of highly functioning elders the remarkable levels of self-reliance, self-esteem, and self-acceptance that they were experiencing. Almost to the person, the group stressed the importance of humor and play for empowering the inner self.

Bianchi found other commonalities. Many of his group

needed to be healed from some painful memories in order to become unstuck from the fruitless repetition of past hurts. Many of the participants had also pursued lifelong education, keeping their minds alert, informed, and challenged.

All of these indicators have a common basis: they must occur in the now. What is real in us can exist only in the present moment.

## We *Can* Choose This Present Moment

Our job as Christians is to perform our function the best we can in the only time that is given to us. That function is to love, and our only time is now. We are to dedicate ourselves to seeing ourselves, as well as our brothers and sisters, as sons and daughters of God who deserve our loving care. When we can genuinely incorporate this love-belief into our attitudinal core and adopt it as our operative perspective, then our present moments extend into forever. As we progress ever closer to achieving this goal, we likewise grow closer to letting go of grudges and grievances. Condemnations such as these serve only to root us in the past with guilt or project fear into our future. When we live with such condemnations, we inject ourselves with the venom of judgment, locking ourselves up in our own self-made prisons. Right now is the time to forgive: allow each present moment to be another link in a chain of loving forgiveness that lasts our entire life. When this is our present-moment goal, the stillness and peace of "now" enfolds us in gentle youthfulness.

Each moment God asks us to learn how to love better. If each morning as we awaken we recite to ourselves, "Today I will learn how to love better," we will open ourselves up more fully to God's generous grace and position ourselves to find success in our day. To learn how to love better, we must focus on the now.

What do we want our "now" to be for us? We have the choice of making this moment whatever we want it to be, whatever is our truth. We can choose to make our present a time of learning and healing, or we can make it a time of turmoil and pain. We can learn to see everything as an extension of the present moment, allowing us to grow from present moment to present moment to present moment, or we can continue to see the present moment as dependent upon what's happened in the past or what might happen in the future. This is a matter of choice. Through prayer and meditation, we can invite the Holy Spirit into our holy "now." When we do this, we take the "now" and extend it into eternity.

Seek to make today the center of your world. Let the past retreat to yesterday, and release the future to tomorrow. You can rest in today, knowing that it is only in the present moment that Christ can comfort you and show you that God is with you always, in the great eternal Now. Here is your peace, here is your love, here is your spiritual vitality, your youthfulness, your agelessness.

# Key 5

---

# Accept Your True Self

*So then you are no longer strangers and aliens, but
you are citizens with the saints and also members of
the household of God....*

Ephesians 2:19

**Key 5 Definition:** The degree to which we come to
know and can genuinely "own" our holy genuine self,
as opposed to our worldly self.

T homas Merton, the noted Trappist monk and interna-
tionally known author, consistently wrote about the distinction between what he called the "true self" and the "false
self." He had different names for these two: spirit self, real
self, genuine self, and others for the true self; the world
self, the ego self, the human self, and so on for the false
self. At first blush this may seem somewhat dualistic, but
what Merton was talking about is spiritual honesty.

For Merton, our real self is that which is aligned with
God and is of God. Because we are all children of God,
God is our first source and center of our being. The degree

to which we understand that this is our true reality far beyond anything that defines us in this world, is the same
degree to which we know ourselves. And we must know
ourselves before we can know God on a personal level.

Each of us is a child of God, a child that yearns, and
sometimes even screams, to come out and express itself
freely. On the back cover of Eugene Bianchi's book *Elder
Wisdom* is a quotation that sums up this notion of spiritual
childhood in a very human way. I think it's quite a statement of integration:

> Eli Wallach (age 78), after a lifetime on stage and in
> films, emphasizes the value of tapping into the inner
> child. During the interview in his New York apartment
> we [Bianchi and assistant] could hear the voices of his
> wife and daughter in another room practicing lines for
> an upcoming performance. It was clearly a household
> of imagination. "You've got to keep imagination and
> emotion alive as an older person," says Wallach, "be-
> cause inside everyone is a child. He's still there in me.
> When I look in the mirror I say, Who is this old guy?
> That's not me. I'm still the young man. Still pulsating.
> Still wanting."

This charming quotation paints a picture of youthfulness
that's both homey and inspirational. For Wallach, being
spiritually integrated and youthful means both pulsating and
still wanting. It's a paradox of sorts that bears some further
examination.

## What Is Maturity?

Youthfulness is that attitudinal quality of vitality, freshness, and honesty that brings color, life, and love to a person regardless of her or his chronological age. Since youthfulness is an attitude, a state of the mind and not a state of the body, we have the power of choosing it. Always. Indeed, as we mature, we become more aware of our own attitudes of youthfulness and infuse them into our belief system in ever more life-giving ways.

Remember what Jesus told us about being a child? Unless we become like children we cannot enter the kingdom of heaven. What is all this talk about children? Are we supposed to go back to a time in our life when we were supposedly immature?

Not by a long shot. The lesson is not to become children, but to become *like* children. In a word, to be ourselves unselfconsciously.

I believe that much of what passes for maturation in our culture is really a process of crystallization. As we become more mature and more logical, do we not also become more crystallized? Logic, of course, is a valuable mental asset, yet logic gives the impression at times of a rather simplistic world, in which everything is either right or wrong. Youthfulness does not deal with life in this way. Youthfulness tempers logic with our emotional reality, with our feelings. As we become more experienced, do we become more like a stone? Or do we become more malleable, more adaptable, more understanding, and more comprehensive in our thinking? Maturity often involves making choices that have as much to do with the logic of the "heart" as with the logic of the "mind."

## Low Self-Esteem Accelerates Aging

One of the key building blocks of spiritual vitality is self-esteem. Have you ever really come to know a person with low self-esteem? Sadly, many persons need only look into a mirror to discover someone with low self-esteem. The simple truth is that people with low self-esteem have not accepted themselves as they are; they think themselves unlovable and so cannot love themselves. People with solid self-esteem, on the other hand, believe deep within themselves that they are worthy, that they are OK, that they are lovable. We are, after all, children of God, made in God's image, so deep down we are good.

Developing self-esteem is an adventure of discovery, for we must learn who we really are, both as a child of God and as an individual human being with particular talents, characteristics, and limitations. Self-knowledge is a challenging desire. Each of us is in a constant state of personal and spiritual evolution. Can we ever really know ourselves completely? Those who are spiritually vital have spent their lifetimes learning who they are, and they deeply love the persons they have come to know.

I think that some of the people who do not age well have decided somewhere along the line, consciously or unconsciously, that they've learned all they need to learn. They've decided who they are as a person and who they're going to be...and that's that! They pride themselves for consistency, for being the same yesterday, today, and tomorrow. Naturally, this sameness they have alighted upon constricts their growth by prematurely shutting off their development; they have closed off their potential and aborted any possibility of being all they can be. In short, they have settled on a definition of themselves that falls short of what God is asking of them. Certainly, this is not a posture that will help us on the road to greater self-understanding, to greater youthfulness, to greater spiritual vitality.

Jack is a retired independent entrepreneur. For years Jack owned and operated a soft-ice-cream shop. Each day at the shop was like the day before for Jack: he seemed unable to inject any sense of adventure, freshness, or vitality into his work. Actually, Jack was endowed with the energy of an adolescent—he seemed like a perpetual-motion dynamo. When he retired, he seemed to simply shift his energy from the crystallized routines of the ice-cream shop to routines around the house. Jack was stuck! He seemed unable to change, to embrace new ideas, new ways of thinking, or new directions for growing. Anthony de Mello might say that Jack was sleepwalking through life.

As a professional counselor I encounter people with low self-esteem every day. Some are angry, some are depressed, but all are in emotional pain, and all are aging at an accelerated rate because an essential element of vitality is evading them. The definition they have of themselves is causing conflict, and they feel the need for change. Many times they point a finger at spouse, parents, or boss, contending that it is all those other people who need to change. They don't know that it is they themselves who need to change. Counseling is a process of changing self, not changing others. A truly mature person realizes this.

Betty suffers from low self-esteem. Thoughts of self-doubt, self-disapproval, and torturous indecision continuously invade her mind. Her initial self-presentation as a "take charge," self-assured person merely hides a deep self-depreciation. She berates her inadequacies with disdain; she emotionally scowls at herself and discounts her sense of personal integrity. She can break into tears so seamlessly that one hardly notices when the tears might begin or end. She seems caught in a trap of personal second-guessing: "Do you think I did the right thing here?...I'm sure someone else could do it much better!..." And so on, in an apparently endless parade of indecision and turmoil. Clearly, Betty's true self is only infrequently given the light of day.

For many and varied reasons, some of us have lost or have never had the opportunity to discover the truth, beauty, and goodness that are inside us. Generally, we have pushed our own needs and desires aside, in deference to those of others. In the process, we may have lost the very essence of ourselves, our wholeness, our personhood. Eventually, we can find ourselves emotionally, and sometimes even spiritually, adrift.

## We Are Citizens of God's Kingdom

We all carry on a dialogue with ourselves. Our thoughts are our internal communication. The old adage *If you talked to other people the way you talk to yourself, you wouldn't have many friends* strikingly portrays the power of positive thinking. What we tell ourselves is important. It determines what we think about ourselves. People with solid self-esteem talk to themselves in positive, confident, and, in the true sense of the word, humble ways.

I believe *the* central ingredient in building self-esteem is our internal dialogue. It is only through the self-expression that occurs within this dialogue that we can come to know who we really are.

This internal dialogue is holy, animated by the Holy Spirit, the Spirit of Truth. The Holy Spirit enables us to learn the truth about our holy self. We need to listen constantly to the voice of calm within, the voice of consistency that whispers no contradictions. When we hear the loving voice of God within and trust in its direction, we will enhance our self-esteem, our vitality, our holiness.

If instead we listen to the world, we will experience conflict and turmoil, self-deception and low self-esteem. A simple question can illustrate the difference. Ask yourself, "Am I first and foremost a body that lives on this material plane and that happens to have a spiritual dimension, or am I first and foremost a spirit that resides within an energy system called a body and that lives together with it on this material plane?" Your answer goes a long way toward illuminating who you are and what you are about in this world. People of the world would say that the body is our true reality. The world may give some recognition to our spiritual nature but would add that it really doesn't matter anyway. On the other hand, people who are searching for celestial honesty would say that we are first and foremost spirit, which happens to be resident in a body.

Christ admonished us to recognize and embrace the reality of God's kingdom and to be mindful always of the transiency of this world. So what is our true self? Our true self, that which is made in the image and likeness of God, is a citizen of God's kingdom, not of this world. This is the self we are to accept, to honor, to own, and to cherish. Here is the truth that releases us from the fears of this world and gives us our identity. Here is the holy message that enables us to live our lives with vitality. Here is the power that gives us the courage to be the unique child of God that we genuinely are.

## Seeing Our Own True Beauty

*Humility* means accepting the truth. Humility does not mean what the world often takes it to mean: self-deprecation and self-denial and even self-injury. Putting self down so that others can feel puffed up is something the world might falsely call self-sacrifice, but it has no redemptive quality, as true sacrifice does. We cannot be humble by denying our true selves, by turning away from the heavenly responsibility of being who it is that God made us to be. It is up to us to grasp the grandeur of our self and celebrate in its awe and beauty because it is this part of us that is perfect, this part of us that is God-like.

I often wonder how Adam and Eve might have understood the virtue of humility? This may be an academic question in itself, but I would like to believe that before the Fall Adam and Eve knew their true identities as children of God. Only after they experienced deception did they lose sight of their true selves.

The fact of the matter is that our true self—what I refer to as our holy self—needs no self-esteem. Our holy self *is* esteem; it is the pure essence of esteem; it is already the life force of the universe, the potency of the heavens, the power of the cosmos. No human foible, mistake, omission, or commission can separate us from the celestial vitality of who we really are. No matter what our sin or transgression, we will always remain a child of God, even though we may not feel like one.

The process of aging enables us to accept our holy self. For as our bodies disintegrate and become less "attractive" according to worldly standards, we begin to search elsewhere for experiences of beauty. And no experience is more beautiful than coming to understand who and what we really are: beloved children of God.

I believe that if we truly came to identify with our holy self, we'd be in such ecstasy at our own truth, beauty, and goodness that we could hardly bear to live in this world. I have a word for this deep internal beauty. I call it *luster,* and I believe it has three component parts.

The first component of our luster is light. We have luminosity; we shine because we are the reflection of God. Part of claiming our holy self is to see our light most clearly. What did Jesus instruct us to do with our light? Put it on a pedestal and let it shine for all to see. He told us not to put it under a bushel basket so that it is covered over, but that's what happens to our luster when we have low self-esteem. Low self-esteem causes us to depreciate ourselves, to discount ourselves, to disbelieve that we are holy. Solid self-esteem lets us allow our true holiness to shine like a beacon on a hill.

The second component of our luster is beauty. At our very core exists an attractiveness that surpasses anything the world can offer. We are called to contact this beauty, to appreciate it, to cherish it, to give testimony to it. We are to do this all in finest humility. If we could see and really accept the beauty of our holy self, we could also grasp the everyday beauty of the life that surrounds us.

The third component of our luster is status. We are God's children. Think of it! We are the highest of any created being in the universe. The angels are not higher; they are made to be the same angels forever. We children of God are called to grow, to change, to come closer to God. Indeed, to become perfect as God is perfect. How fantastic! I believe if we could truly comprehend our status among creation, we would quickly come to find worldly things completely trivial. We would become disinterested in material possessions, professional success, wealth, and so forth. Enthralled in our "child of God" status and exalted in our newly found distinctiveness, we would enter an altered state of consciousness that would be close to ecstasy.

Our daily task is simply to become aware of our luster. If each moment we see the beauty that lies inside us, accept the truth of who and what we really are, and embrace the goodness that made us in God's image, we will find ourselves following the light of Christ as he leads us to God. Our life is a journey both purposeful and intentional, and it is full of lessons of love for us to learn every day, the foremost of which is to know who we truly are.

## The 5 Spiritual Access Tools

Practically speaking, how can we become aware of our luster? There are five practical ways, which I call the 5 Spiritual Access Tools: prayer, meditation, drawing, storywriting, and journaling. Each will help you better access and more clearly own your holy self.

The first, of course, is prayer. Through prayer we connect ourselves with the eternal that is right inside of us, and speaking to God daily is essential. Each day, confide in your internal teacher, the Holy Spirit within, who stands ready to offer guidance, hope, and light. Gradually, you will grow ever closer to living your life as God intended, in peace, love, and balance.

The second tool is spiritual meditation. By meditation I mean taking an issue, an event, a relationship, or an occurrence and connecting it in a very centered, peaceful way with the glory of God. It's speaking to God, but more important it's listening to God.

The third way of becoming aware of your holy self is through drawing. In drawing, you will move beneath the conscious level and access your subconscious or preconscious existence. You don't have to be Rembrandt; for spiritual purposes, anyone can draw. And you can draw anything: your inner child, your holy self, your aging, your patience. You can draw yourself tending the garden of your soul to bring forth more luscious fruit. You can draw what you're learning from this thing called aging.

Story-writing is another avenue into your holy self. Once again, you're accessing part of yourself that isn't readily accessible on a conscious level. Even if you don't understand what you're writing about yourself, you will still benefit from it. Place yourself at the center of the story; become the hero or heroine. Write about how you feel as the plot develops. Write about what you observe, or what you desire, or what you enjoy. (Story-writing and drawing are also great tools for those who work with seniors of any age.)

The fifth vehicle is journaling, keeping a record of your spiritual insights. Perhaps daily, perhaps every other day, keep a record of the kinds of feelings you're having. Write down your observations about yourself and your relationships, paying particularly close attention to your relationship with God. Be sure to record both the "good" and the "bad" feelings. Over time, as you reread your journal, you will discern patterns in the fabric of your life. Only when you understand what the patterns are will you know what changes you might need to make.

I urge you to try these tools, either one at a time or in combination. You may be astonished at the discoveries you will begin making about yourself. It may sometimes be rough going, but becoming acquainted with your holy self will be well worth your effort.

## The Mirror

The symbol for the fifth key, acceptance of your real self, is a mirror. Because they reflect images, mirrors symbolize our own self-reflection. Just like Eli Wallach says when he looks in the mirror, "Who is this old man reflected back in the mirror?" we can also fail to recognize our reflected image. When we look in the mirror, what do we see? If all we see is our physical body, we're missing the point of what living is all about, because we're failing to see who we really are and to realize the true growth that is open to us right now.

As we get closer to our inner self and come to accept it as our true self, we will gradually realize that our ego, the social mask we wear every day for the people around us, is not who we truly are. We will come to know the image of our true self is so much more than the bodily image reflected in the bathroom mirror. Our true reality is *transform*, beyond the material level. When we revel in our holy self, we will be truly open to God's transforming power.

# Key 6

---

# Forgive Others and Self

*So when you are offering your gift at the altar, if you remember that your brother or sister has something against you, leave your gift there before the altar and go; first be reconciled to your brother or sister, and then come and offer your gift.*

Matthew 5:23–24

**Key 6 Definition:** The degree to which we can learn the essentials of forgiveness and bring forgiveness into practice in our life.

## Body-Mind-Spirit Connection

I open the discussion of the sixth key to spiritual vitality with a question: What does the body-mind-spirit connection have to do with forgiveness? I leave the answer to the late Norman Cousins, editor of the *Saturday Review* for thirty years, who devoted the last twelve years of his life to amassing all the scientific research that substantiated the connection between the mind and the body. In his seventy-

71

fourth year he wrote, "Certainly we ought not grant others the right to give us ulcers." In this simple yet profound statement Cousins captured the practical benefits of Christian forgiveness.

We don't really understand how stimulation of the mind biologically, chemically, or electrically transforms the body, yet the connection between the body and the mind seems well documented. There are mountains of hard medical data now that connect the workings of the body with the thoughts and feelings of mind. And the case histories seem incontrovertible.

I vividly remember the day a thirty-four-year-old man walked into my counseling office. He remains for me the premier example of the clinical need for forgiveness. He was an accountant referred by his surgeon, who had just taken out three-fourths of the man's stomach. It had become so perforated with ulcers that even the surgeon assumed that something must be wrong with this young man's life.

I interviewed the man, and it became obvious to me that he didn't have what we would generally consider to be an accountant's personality. As a matter of fact, I gave him a personality profile called a *Myers Briggs Type Indicator* personality test, and he turned out to be the same personality type as me! This was flabbergasting, as I would have expected the personality type of an accountant to be different from that of a Christian counselor. I'm sure there are similarities, but we would naturally think that these two professions would draw quite different personality types. So I was prompted to ask him a question: "How is it you became an accountant?" To which he answered, "My mother thought it was a good idea."

Why do I bring up this example? This man clearly needed to offer forgiveness. At first, I thought he needed to forgive his father. What I didn't realize was his equally pressing need to forgive his mother. The history of his family of origin helped to explain why. This man was an oldest child. His father was emotionally absent from the family much of the time. From my interview with this man, it became clear that he had what is commonly called a "coalition" relationship with his mother. This had developed during his formative years. Because of his father's emotional absence, the son had become the emotional mainstay for his mother. She relied too much on him, and the emotional impact continued to ripple through his life.

A coalition is an exceedingly close relationship. The only coalition that's supposed to exist in a family is the one between father and mother, husband and wife. When we find coalitions in the family other than between the parents, we look more closely for family problems. If we see a coalition relationship between a mother and a son particularly, or a father and a daughter, we are then clued in to the strong possibility that something is amiss in the family. Something was contorting this family into an imbalanced relationship configuration.

This man's mother was looking for emotional security in her son because she couldn't find it with her own husband. So she transferred her desires onto her own son. His mother worked for—you guessed it—an accountant. She couldn't think of a more stable profession than that of accountant. The dutiful son followed suit.

Certainly, this mother is not to blame; she acted as she thought she needed to act. From my clinical experience, I believe that we are entirely too hard on our parents. I would say that there are really very few things that a person must believe or do in this world in order to be mentally healthy. However, chief among these things is that we must come to believe that our parents did their best.

Some of the patients with whom I deal say that this can't be true because their mother or father wasn't nearly as good as Mrs. Murphy or Mrs. Zukowski or Mr. Costello or Mr. Perez who lived down the street. They protest that their parents couldn't have done their best. "How could you say that my parents did their best?" they retort. My response is always the same: "You got your parents' best. You cannot compare your parents to anybody who lived down the street or on the next block. They did their best for you." They may come back with, "Well, my mother really loved my sister better." And I would say, "Ask your sister what she thinks." With all that our parents may have on their shoulders, including their relationship with their own parents, we are forced to believe that we all got the best from our mother and father. However meager or possibly abusive it might have been, it was still their best.

The reason I say this so strongly is that if you believe anything else, what's your conclusion? "I wasn't loved." "I didn't receive what I needed." "I was misunderstood." We now have an emotional excuse. We may not even be aware of this consciously, but we can use it as a way to dull or avoid our own spiritual development. In other words, when we're pointing a finger someplace else, we're not taking responsibility for our own life.

Getting back to the body-mind-spirit connection: by working as an accountant, my patient with the ulcers was stuffing his feeling of unknown unforgiveness to such a degree that he was at war with himself. His turmoil was manifested in his body; he took his emotional conflict and somaticized it. To *somaticize* means taking an emotional issue and unconsciously displacing it onto our own bodies. In this man's case the somatization found a target in his stomach and eventually required drastic surgery to remedy.

I'm happy to report that although the man is still an accountant, he has changed his practice dramatically. You see, what he was doing was crunching numbers in front of a computer all day. A person with a personality like his shouldn't have been doing that because it would give him an ulcer—and another one, and another one after that. He's now expanded his practice and hired two very clever persons who enjoy sitting in front of computers and crunching numbers all day. And he goes out and has lunch with his clients. This is what he really wants to do.

Norman Cousins titled his final book *Head First: The Biology of Hope and the Healing Power of the Human Spirit.* Did you ever think that hope was biological? Cousins says sickness, either physical or mental, is the result of many things, not least among them our mental attitudes. Our thirty-four-year-old man was afflicted with ulcers not simply because of what he put into his stomach, but also because of what he put into his mind. Relationships with family and friends, ambitions, hopes and fears, worldly expectations, and much, much more all get transformed into our own biology.

Some years ago I took note of a cartoon in a magazine that I have never forgotten. It showed a picture of a president of a large corporation. He is saying, "Ulcers! I don't get ulcers…I give them." Norman Cousins tells us that we ought not let others have the right to give us ulcers. How do we protect ourselves, then, from this kind of tragedy? I would say that forgiveness is probably the premier way of protection for a Christian. Let's take a closer look at this.

## Germs of Ill Health

I remember a client who looked about ten or fifteen years older than his age. Time after time, our counseling sessions would end up in the same place, a discussion of how awful his father had treated him as a boy. In point of fact, his father was emotionally abusive to his son, who was now my patient. Even if only half of what the son was telling me was true, it was clear that the father was an abusive man.

But my patient was making a career out of discounting his father. If I had let him, this counselee would have droned on and on about his father's abuse. As Shakespeare wrote, "He doth protest too much." I had the sense that my patient's need to berate his father interminably was also an attempt on his part to forfeit personal responsibility for his own life, which was seriously out-of-balance at the time. This pattern of blame only served to infect this man with a terrible turmoil and prevented him from really moving ahead in his life.

Blame, judgment, criticism, resentment, brooding, anger: these are the vehicles of ill health, the thieves of our vitality. How much more rapidly do we age when these are our daily emotional diet? What stagnation of spirit and invasions of the body do these aliens produce as they poison our peace of mind? When we embrace these destructive villains, and mistakenly take them on for our defense, we unknowingly impair our ability to withstand disease. These are the germs of ill health, germs that spread poisons within us and prevent our spiritual garden from growing.

Eventually, I'm happy to report, my client was able to embrace a semblance of forgiveness of his father. This didn't solve all his problems, but it did bring perhaps the biggest gift that he had ever received: peace of mind. I often wonder if this peace of mind allowed him to carry on in life, but I have found in my studies that people who can forgive live much more gracious, integrated, and satisfied lives than those who do not.

## Never Cease Forgiving

When Peter asked Jesus how often he should forgive a brother who sins against him, Jesus answered, "seventy-seven times" (Matthew 18:22). Here was our Master's view of the value of forgiveness. Forgive always, and never cease forgiving. Is this humanly possible? To answer this question, we need to understand the meaning of forgiveness.

We sometimes think and talk about forgiveness as if it were something we could do on a Sunday afternoon while drinking lemonade. But forgiveness is very hard. Make no mistake about it. It may seem strange to put it this way, but we can't forgive. We don't have that power. Only God can forgive, and God has already forgiven us and everyone else for whatever transgressions we may be guilty. Quite regularly in my counseling practice I will hear someone say, "I just can't forgive myself." My response is always a question: *Do you think that God has forgiven you?* To a person the people who can't forgive themselves respond, "Well, of course God has forgiven me!"

Do we sometimes place ourselves on some illusionary pedestal of righteousness, trying to measure up to some perfectionistic standard of behavior? Does this standard outstrip even God's? We need to become more keenly aware of constructing illogical standards that impede our forgiveness and keep us prisoners of a contorted logic. The only thing we are called to do is to open ourselves to the potential of forgiveness. We are continuously called to find the willingness to forgive.

## Forgiveness Is Not...

We harbor some rather distorted views about forgiveness, and one way to gain a clearer understanding of forgiveness is to look at what forgiveness is not. First, forgiveness does not mean that we excuse an offender from responsibility for his or her action. All of us want to be just, but we think that when we forgive someone, we're offering them some sort of justification for what they've done. We absurdly think that our forgiveness somehow conveys the message that what they did was OK. Carrying such thinking to its illogical conclusion, we bind ourselves into a paralyzed state of unforgiveness because we can't tell them that their offense was not an offense. So we don't forgive. But forgiveness really has nothing whatsoever to do with the nature of the violation. On the contrary, forgiveness means deciding to give up resentment, ceasing to feel you have claim to any recompense for some offense, real or imagined. Forgiveness means blessing the offender and recognizing the "offense" as a lesson in love. The main point is that we forgive not to "let the other guy off the hook" but rather to bring the mighty gift of peace of mind into our own life once again. We are the recipient of the benefits of our choice to forgive.

Second, forgiveness is not something that requires the

offending party to claim remorse and make amends. Sometimes we put up conditions that the "offending" person must satisfy if we are to forgive her. "Well, I would be glad to forgive my sister if she'd just apologize to me…if she just gave my son the money that she borrowed from him ten years ago…if she visited mom's grave more often…went to church…turned purple…." We want the other person to pay, so we conjure up conditions, and we're right back to "an eye for an eye and a tooth for a tooth." Such "logic" is certainly not forgiveness. Rather, it's a deal that you're making. "Well, if you apologize, I'll forgive you." That's the same as saying, "If you give me $150,000, I'll give you my house." It's really sort of ridiculous when you look at it that way, yet we feel the need to make things "even." What are we really doing here? We're tying ourselves up. We're holding onto our unforgiveness and ensuring that our morning poison gets mixed in with our coffee. This is not what Jesus taught us. Rather, he told us, if we have something against our neighbor, we should leave whatever it is we are doing, even if we're approaching the altar of God, and go make it up with that person. We should take the initiative and forgive, he taught, for our own sake, without expecting anything in return.

Third, and in a related way, forgiveness is not an admission that we were "wrong." Naturally, we all like to be right. But when people have the false idea that forgiving is somehow an admission of guilt, and when they have a self-concept that cannot tolerate anything but being right, they will be unable to forgive anyone anything. But more than that, the need to be right all the time is a tremendous psychological burden; it saps energy we could use more productively. When we stand on our own "rightness" as if we were

the sole caretaker of righteousness, we are putting ourselves
in dire peril. It's like holding a razor blade to our heart and
taking little slices out of our ourselves every time we have
to be right. Eventually, we become anemic and sick. I like
what psychiatrist and author Dr. Gerald Jampolsky, M.D.,
says in his book *Say Goodbye to Guilt.* He asks, "Would
you rather be right or would you rather be happy?" Although
rightness and happiness are not mutually exclusive, the one
clearly does not always produce the other.

Fourth, forgiveness is not reconciliation. Some of us actually bundle them together as though the two were the same.
It would be "nice" for us to reconcile every time we forgave someone else, and reconciliation is sometimes possible; at other times it certainly is not. Often, we would like
to forgive someone, but because we don't want to be "buddy-
buddy" with him or her, we put off forgiveness, thinking it
inseparable from friendship. We need to unbundle reconciliation from forgiveness; indeed, the other doesn't
necessarily need to know that we are forgiving them. Forgiveness is really between ourselves and God. When it
is we who need to make amends, however, then we clearly
need to let the other person know.

## Unconditional Forgiveness

Either our thoughts are of love—and, therefore, of forgiveness—or they are critical, blaming, and judgmental; there
is no middle ground. Yet much of our forgiveness is condi-
tional—that is, we require certain conditions before we can
move to forgive. "Right" may be on our side—legally, morally, ethically, financially, or in any other way—but when
we refuse to let go of revenge, however faintly we may

harbor it, we still block ourselves from fully enjoying our life and our health.

Unconditional forgiveness, which has no "strings" nor other conditions, is forgiveness in its purest form. Certainly, we would all like to believe ourselves capable of this type of forgiveness. In reality, however, unconditional forgiveness is not only elusive, it may also be quite humanly impossible. Thinking "perfect" unconditional forgiveness the only kind of forgiveness God finds acceptable can hinder us from taking the first steps toward developing the willingness to forgive.

We can never become perfectly patient, nor perfectly charitable, nor perfectible merciful—at least not on this material plane. The virtues of patience, charity, and mercy exist in their purest state in God, not in us. Paradoxically, we *are* called to pursue these virtues here on earth, to become perfect like God. Can we approach forgiveness in the same way? Seldom, if ever, can we walk on the outer edges of full unconditional forgiveness, but we can move in that direction, as we *are* called to do.

## Principles for Forgiveness

As noted author Deepak Chopra, M.D., writes in his book *Ageless Body, Timeless Mind: The Quantum Alternative to Growing Old,* "Forgiveness of others comes only when you can release your own hurt. The more complete your release the more sincere your forgiveness." Our own unforgiveness confines us to a terrible path, a path of pain, and we struggle to avoid the perils that lie there. What we fail to recognize is that the terrible obstacles on the path come from our own hurting, our own unforgiveness that we're projecting onto somebody else. As long as we project it elsewhere, we will continue to experience this awful pain blocking our way to happiness. This can even become our "norm"; we will learn to live with it, and soon we won't even notice how we are hobbling along through life, because this is how we've always lived. As Dr. Chopra explains, we stop feeling our own hurts, but we need to feel them again so that we can be released from them.

How often I hear from my patients, "I'd like to forgive, but I don't know how." How do we unburden ourselves through forgiveness so that we can achieve peace? Here are four principles that can help you learn forgiveness:

The first principle is to accept whatever part of the responsibility for the "offense" may be rightfully yours. Pointing fingers, blaming others, and absolving ourselves of everything is easy, but oftentimes some measure of responsibility belongs to us. We need to accept our part in it.

I find this first principle violated often between marriage partners. One partner will outline an "offense" committed by the other. This will be described in detail and in a tone of voice that only underscores the insensitivity of the "offending partner"—and the complete innocence of the "victim." However, when the "offending partner" explains the events leading up to the supposed "offense" and the surrounding circumstances and behaviors, the entire picture becomes much clearer. Responsibility seldom, if ever, lies wholly with one partner. Indeed, the "offense" may even seem a logical behavior under the illuminated circumstances.

Leon admonishes his wife, Sara, for her incessant "hounding" of him. He claims that she calls him at work three and four times a day, having him paged off the factory floor where he is a supervisor. He offers these "transgressions" as obvious testimony that Sara is insecure and dependent upon him, and he appears to resent it. When the full picture is exposed, however, everyone realizes that Leon has neglected to take responsibility for his part in Sara's "transgressions." Leon also calls Sara three and four times a day, always ending the conversation with "Call me when you get a chance." In fact, there appears to be a dependent coalition between Leon and Sara, one that evidently serves several psychological purposes.

The second principle of forgiveness is to examine any long-term grudges objectively. I've known people, and probably you have too, who are angry and unforgiving toward other members of their family, but who don't even know why they became angry in the first place. They've been angry for such a long time that they've completely forgotten the infraction that originally caused the grudge they're holding. They keep holding onto unforgiveness because they don't know what else to do.

If you are angry with your sister for some terrible thing that happened years ago, can you objectively examine your role now in this ongoing feud? You may say, "Well, I don't have any part in it at all. What she did was no fault of mine. It hurt me terribly, and it still hurts me to think about it." This may be the truth of the matter. However, if you didn't have a part in the creation of the grudge, you can still have a part in its extension. When we are unable to let go of an affront, we give it power over us. We let it begin to control our feelings and our reactions. We have a role in it now.

It's hard to forgive, but it's almost impossible to forget. Many of us harbor a notion that we must forget in order to forgive. This is simply erroneous. Jesus never asked us to forget. He did, however, ask us over and over to forgive, and to forgive again and again. Forgetting may mean repressing, denying, or using some other psychological gymnastic to somehow push the hurting away. This can be detrimental to our own mental wellness because it prevents us from resolving the issue. Left unattended within us, whatever grudge we may be carrying will fester and grow. But if we bring it to the light of day and work with it in God's time, the hurting will diminish, and we will eventually be able to forgive.

The third forgiveness principle is to recognize that forgiveness is an active decision to love. We need to see forgiveness as active. Forgiveness doesn't happen on it's own. It does not simply descend upon us one day, effortlessly lifting the burden of grudge from us. We have to work at it. We have to decide that we want to forgive, and we have to develop a willingness to forgive, even if our feelings are so strong that we cannot forgive right now. We must say to ourselves, "I wish to develop the willingness to forgive." Here is the first giant step toward being able to forgive someone else.

It may take weeks, months, maybe even years to develop the full willingness needed to begin the forgiveness process. It may take prayer, meditation, education, counseling, journaling. It may take all kinds of things to become like the merciful master who forgave each of his debtors a generous measure of their debt (see Matthew 18:23–35). Forgiving, however, is an extension of God's love, and when we extend God's love to others, we know God's love within ourselves too.

The fourth principle is to look upon the "offender" through the eyes of Christ. Everyone is a child of God, beloved of God regardless of his or her behaviors and thus innately deserving of your love. So we have to ask ourselves the question *How would Christ see this?* This is really an extension of the second key of spiritual vitality, "seek love everywhere." If we ask ourselves, "Where is the love in this particular 'offense'?" we may be surprised to find ourselves feeling empathy for the "offender." Why did your brother say what he did at your son's wedding five years ago? In your eyes he made you look like a fool in front of all your friends and relatives. He didn't even seem to notice your embarrassment. Why did he do that? Well, maybe he just wanted to be more powerful. Maybe he just wanted to show off. Maybe he was just joking around as he always does and didn't realize how hurtful his jokes were. Here is an invitation for us to see this situation differently, to see it as Christ would. If we can do that, if we can come to feel love toward an "offender," then forgiveness will follow almost automatically.

In summary:

1. Accept responsibility if you have been partially to blame.
2. Stop holding grudges.
3. Make an active decision to love.
4. Look with the eyes of Christ.

Throughout this chapter, you may have thought that the only forgiveness I've been talking about is forgiveness toward others. But you and I have just as great a need to forgive ourselves for our own "trespasses." Many times I have encountered people who are blaming themselves for not having been the good children they think they should have been, for not having been the student they should have been,

for not being the parent, or teacher, or spouse, or sibling, or
Christian they should be. Such self-incrimination drops the
weight of unforgiveness directly onto ourselves—with tremendously detrimental effect. Forgiving ourselves is perhaps even more difficult than forgiving others, but it is even
more necessary to our well-being. Everything that we've
just outlined may be best devoted to ourselves first.

## Practical Benefits of Forgiveness

What are the benefits of forgiveness? What can we expect
as a consequence of developing a forgiving nature?

First, forgiveness stimulates your spiritual growth. As a
matter of fact, without forgiveness there will be little, if
any, spiritual growth. Unforgiveness stops our spiritual
growth in its tracks; it takes a lot of energy not to forgive.
By letting go of the crushing weight of blame, we can release energy formerly trapped in the unproductive service
of holding a grudge and unleash it for our use in more
growthful and vitalizing ways. Holding a grudge is hard
work; it saps our vitality and stamina, leaving us spiritually
lifeless and emotionally numb.

Second, forgiveness releases energy that you are otherwise wasting by holding onto unforgiveness. Mostly we've
been talking about blaming other people, but the number
one person we blame, the number one person we don't forgive, is ourself. Forgiveness carries the promise that we
will be purified if we confess our sins and seek forgiveness
(1 John 1:9). This promise brings with it the peace that passes
all human understanding.

Third, forgiveness allows you to live more abundantly.
As Norman Cousins writes in *Head First,* "I have learned

that life is an adventure in forgiveness. Nothing clutters the soul more than remorse, resentment, and recrimination." Beyond cluttering our souls, Cousins continues, remorse, resentment, and recrimination will paralyze our entire immune system, our number one defense against sickness, at least temporarily. Forgiveness can awaken our immune system again.

## The Bridge

The symbol of this sixth key is a bridge. Condemnation, judgment, fault, and blame pollute the waters that flow between us and the life God intended us to live. Forgiveness is our bridge over these unhealthy waters. When we forgive, we are crossing over pain, distrust, and fear. When we forgive, we are allowing the beauty, truth, and goodness within each of us to burst back into life. We are allowing ourselves to "take heart" (Matthew 9:2).

# Key 7

---

# Let Go of Anger and Other Inner Turmoil

*Shun youthful passions and pursue righteousness, faith, love, and peace, along with those who call on the Lord from a pure heart.*

2 Timothy 2:22

**Key 7 Definition:** The degree to which we feel peace of mind and a sense of God's love in our heart.

## Anger Is a Mature Human Emotion

Doesn't this definition sound wonderful? Who among us would not want to feel peace of mind and a sense of God's love in our hearts? Anger and other inner turmoil can stop us from feeling this. So it might seem strange to realize that anger is a mature human emotion. Did Jesus ever show anger? He certainly seemed angry the day in the Temple when he threw out the money changers. That must have been quite a scene. Can't you picture him flinging those tables aside, all those coins rolling across the floor, clanging here and there?

What he did must have caused a lot of anger among the money changers as well. They had been carrying on their trade for a long time, and their fathers before them, and their grandfathers before them. Money changing was a form a banking in ancient Jerusalem. Devout Jews would come from all over to visit the Temple. They would need to exchange their foreign money, as was required by Jewish law so that they could enter the Temple. All of this was quite acceptable.

But Christ showed a lot of anger, didn't he? He shouted—and he became somewhat "manic" at that—"My house should be a house of prayer, not a den of thieves."

Let me ask you a question. How long do you think it was before the money changers were back? As soon as Jesus left, you think—maybe that afternoon, maybe the next morning? So you think the money changers did come back? Is it written anywhere in Scripture that Jesus went back to throw out the money changers a second time? No! I think there's a vital lesson for us about anger in this case.

Anger is an important human emotion; its purpose, like that of all strong emotions, is motivation. Anger can motivate us to action that we ordinarily wouldn't take or to express emotion that we would normally keep within. So anger can be beneficial. Jesus was angry with the money changers and the Temple hierarchy because they were teaching people to seek things of this world, not God and spiritual things. And his anger motivated him to do something that would serve as a better lesson. My sense is that when he was overturning the money tables, he knew the money changers would be back. He wasn't trying to change Jerusalem's economic system, he was making a point. I think we'd all agree that time has proven Jesus' use of anger in this case magnificently effective.

There are other reasons for anger besides the expression of genuine emotions, and we need to understand them if we are to develop the capacity to control our anger and use it as a positive motivational force that it is intended to be.

The second reason for anger is to protect ourselves from closeness with others. This may seem paradoxical—why would we want to be protected from closeness with others?—but it makes sense psychologically. Were you to attempt to be close to a person you've just met, you'd be taking a big risk because you'd be opening yourself up to rejection. The risk is even greater for Sheila, however, because in the past she's felt the sting of rejection from people she's wanted to befriend. To insulate herself against the possibility of rejection again, Sheila uses anger to keep everybody at arm's distance.

Another reason for anger is to alter the behavior of other people. Our subconscious might reflect, "I don't like what you're doing, so I'm going to get big and bold and I'm going to bully you with my anger so you'll change your way of doing things. Because I don't like it." Many of us have seen anger working in this way, and we may use it similarly. As long as we stay angry with Joe, he will probably never again do what made us angry in the first place, because if he does we'll get even angrier with him. In other words, we make him scared of us.

We also use anger to disguise other feelings, particularly feelings of hurt. I like to say, "If you scratch an angry person, what you find underneath the scratch is hurt." Gail was emotionally wounded long ago; as a consequence, today she builds the "Great Wall of Anger" between herself and other people for protection. It works very well, and no one dares approach her, let alone hurt her, because her anger keeps them away.

Anger can disguise alienation and communicate that we don't even care. Dennis, new on the job, just wants to have lunch with someone, but he finds that no one has an empty seat for him in the cafeteria. "Who wants to be with those people anyway. They're just a bunch of jerks," Dennis might say to himself. You see how he is using anger? To justify his feelings about being pushed away and alienated.

Standing up for our rights is another reason for anger. When people become angry about discrimination or pollution, for example, they protest, they rally, they write letters—they take action. Sometimes it goes overboard. In our culture, people focus their anger through litigation. They've already talked themselves into believing that they deserve what they demand. You've heard of the robber who was robbing the pharmacy? He fell through the skylight during the burglary. Then he sued the pharmacist because he believed he had a right to rob that pharmacy without getting injured.

Anger can be an effective tool for expressing what you want, for pushing for our own "shoulds and oughts," as long as anger is not our only tool. All of us believe that some things need to be changed. We can become righteously indignant—that is, angry in a constructive way—or we can allow ourselves to use our anger about a particular situation to dump all of our long-held emotional "baggage." Some people will save up all those little hurts in their backpacks, surveying the horizon to find that one place where they can say, "Aha! Here is where I can dump all of my anger along with all this other junk that I've carried around for so long." Have you ever been on the receiving end of such action? You scratch your head and say, "What's going on here? This is certainly a lot more intense than this situation warrants."

It has been said that anger is a mature human emotion when it doesn't last more than five minutes and doesn't hurt anyone. The five-minute time limit is only figurative. If we let anger become part of our inner life, it ceases to be constructive anger and become a grudge. Likewise, the goal of anger is not to attack people but to express our sentiments in an effort to bring about some beneficial change. The lesson Jesus taught us about anger through the incident in the Temple is that anger is justified when it has a specific goal and/or purpose, it stays within our conscious control (that it, we know we are angry but don't let our anger control us), it's over very quickly, and it doesn't hurt anybody.

## The Manhole Cover

Who among us would deliberately force ourselves to age unnaturally quickly? Probably no one in their right mind. Yet that is exactly what holding onto anger does—it accelerates our aging process. When we protract our anger by saying to ourselves, "No, I will not give up my anger…they don't deserve my love," we are letting our anger control us. And as we read in the previous chapter, retained anger creates in us a spirit of unforgiveness that is quite unhealthy.

When we refuse to let go of our anger, we place ourselves smack on top of a pressurized manhole cover. Imagine that the manhole cover is a lid on all the angry emotions you've been stuffing for a long time. The pressure has mounted gradually. When you deposited that first shred of anger into the hole, the cover was easy to hold down; very little pressure had formed, and you needed very little energy to keep it in. As the years progressed and you stuffed more and more anger into the hole, the pressure grew. You found that keeping all that anger beneath your manhole cover consumed almost all of your energy. You became exhausted, ragged, and depressed because there seemed no end in sight. The energy needed to keep your anger going, and keep your lid on, is almost inconceivable. It's easy to understand why a manhole cover is the symbol for the seventh key to spiritual vitality.

## Anger and Fear

Anger hastens the aging process. Anger that is held within, day after day, for year after year, wears us down. It is a toxic force within our energy system. Certainly, anger hastens the aging process in many different ways. I would like to quote again from Deepak Chopra's book *Ageless Body, Timeless Mind*. In it he writes, "No one really hurts you unless you give them the power to do so. This power lies in your own unresolved pain. You can take control of your own pain and claim power over your emotions. Until you do that, your feelings will continue to be tossed around at the whim of others." We can have power over our anger. To what degree are we giving that power away?

In my counseling practice I encounter many people who are full of fear. Their fear may manifest itself in many different ways, from an inability to choose a seat at church or at the movies to an inability to enter malls, drive on highways, cross over bridges. The strange ways in which anxiety makes its presence felt are too numerous and varied to enumerate. We clinically call this *agoraphobia:* fear of being in public places.

What is the basis of agoraphobia? Generally, the reason for the fear resides not in the outside world, but in our inside world. And one of the things that I think people become afraid of is their own anger. They've held onto their anger and stopped themselves from expressing it. They've never turned over the money tables in the Temple, figuratively speaking. They've sat on that manhole cover and trapped every sniff of anger inside. Many times they were taught to bury their anger, often because anger, when it finally blows off the manhole cover, can be destructive. "A good boy is never angry. A good girl never shows her anger." So it's not their fault that they have to unlearn a bad lesson and embrace a healthier way of dealing with anger.

People can become afraid of their own anger, but it's also true that anger is an emotional response arising from fear. We experience anger whenever we are preparing to "fight" another. Usually, this "fight response" occurs when we recognize a threat of some kind. Anthropologists tell us that early humans were able to adapt to the many threats in their world by developing an extremely quick "fight or flight" response. When danger presented itself—let's say a wild animal was about to attack—our early ancestors quickly sized up the situation and decided whether the best chance of survival was to stand and fight the beast or to flee from the scene as fast as possible. In either case, fighting or fleeing, the entire body and mind immediately prepared to expend high amounts of energy. Every bodily system rallied together, providing the energy to fight like a tiger or run like a deer. The heart raced, glucose flooded into the bloodstream, blood vessels expanded, hormones of all kinds sloshed through the veins, the nervous system went into hyperalert, digestion stopped, sweat glands expanded, and the immune system temporarily suspended activity. The entire body was instantly placed in a state of maximum readiness to meet the crisis.

In our modern world, we seldom meet with wild beasts, but we are stressed in many other ways, and the "fight or flight" response is still operative in us. Whenever we feel anger and prepare to defend ourselves, or when we become fearful and want to avoid a situation, our body prepares itself in exactly the same way our early ancestors' bodies did when facing that wild animal.

When we do this over and over again, our body's ability to respond quickly and intensely begins to wane. Our body gradually loses the effectiveness it once had. Here is the aging process in action. By keeping us in a perpetual state of hyperreadiness for attack, unresolved anger drains our vitality down to nothing.

A grudge is particularly harmful because it is a combination of the fighting response and the fleeing response. Holding a grudge keeps us in a continuous state of readiness to either attack or flee—we don't know which, and this impairs our body's ability to carry on normally. So all our physical, emotional, psychological, mental, and spiritual systems remain so overloaded that they become paralyzed. This opens us up to increased incidence of sickness and vastly accelerates our aging. Holding a grudge is like bathing in a tub of aging; it is the opposite of the fountain of youth.

Grudges also separate us from our true spiritual reality. When we harbor unforgiveness in our heart for long periods, we render ourselves deaf to the voice of God within. The judgment that is in every grudge separates us from God. When we let go of a grudge, we release the formerly constricted spiritual forces within us and reconnect with God.

In the parable of the Compassionate Master and the Unforgiving Servant, the master learned that the servant whose debt he had forgiven was now demanding repayment from others. So the master handed the servant over to the torturers until he should pay back the whole of the original debt. When we remain unforgiving of heart, we too will be delivered over to our own inner tormentors: guilt, shame, fear, and malice will weigh heavily upon us and rob us of our vitality.

## Especially for Women

In our culture, women are socialized very clearly not to show anger. "Ladies" are supposed to tolerate, swallow, project, or do anything with anger except show it. This prohibition on expressing anger gets even more stringent during the later years because our culture tells us that "older women" are supposed to be gracious, motherly, kind, perhaps somewhat submissive, and above all exceedingly adaptable to any and all forces that come their way. The extreme prohibition on anger is sometimes only heightened in good Christian families.

Many Christian women struggle with being not just a "good" woman but a "virtuous" woman. Certainly, there is everything right with being virtuous, yet when the definition of *virtuous* irrationally extends to the repression of any negative emotion, especially anger, we see unwanted behavioral consequences. If a Christian woman, as the rea-

soning goes, shows any anger, it means that she's not virtuous, she's not a good example, she's not even a good person. She ends up feeling repressed and contorted, unable to
grow maximally.

I will tell you that for every male client feeling anxiety I
have probably seven or eight female clients who come in
expressing anxiety. The cultural prohibition against anger
and other negative emotions clearly has something to do
with this lopsided incidence of anxiety symptoms.

What our culture teaches women with regards to anger is
inappropriate, and it is something I call an *antique belief.*
It's a belief that once had value but doesn't have validity,
credibility, or utility in our lives any longer; it's an artifact
of a previous life stage.

Harriet Lerner, in her most interesting book *The Dance
of Anger,* addresses this issue of antique beliefs. What she
expresses is quite important for women in general and Christian women in particular. She describes two common responses that women can have to the repression of anger
required by this antique belief. The first she calls the *nice-
lady* response. Some women adopt a nice-lady approach to
living when they cover up their anger, denying it and never
allowing themselves to feel it directly. They behave with
impeccable graciousness, project a seamless exterior of calm
and dignity, and simply ignore or dismiss all the complexi-
ties of life. These women are pleasant, wonderful, and un-
ruffled. Nothing affects them negatively. They seem to have
a highly efficient internal disposal system that flushes away
any kind of negative emotion or anger. They are simply
nice ladies.

At the other end of the spectrum, the other response
Lerner calls the *bitchy-lady* response. A woman who adopts

this mechanism for dealing with anger is also known as "The Nag." Such a woman expresses anger, or is upset, about absolutely everything. She lets everyone around her know that nothing is ever right. And, for her, nothing can ever be right. This woman is generally unpleasant and can make life miserable for everyone else.

Now we might think that these are two diametrically opposed responses to living and to expressing emotions. Harriet Lerner would tell us otherwise. She would say they're very much the same because neither one of these responses allows a woman to genuinely express what she really feels inside. Neither the nice lady nor the bitchy lady expects any change to occur, and neither communicates a genuine seriousness about the desire for things to be any different. The nice lady never expresses a need for any change. Because the bitchy lady says that everything needs to be changed, nothing will be. These women are angry, but they are not assertive; they are not serious about wanting change.

## How to Let Go

Anger will always seek expression; if it can't find expression in the outside world, most likely the repressed anger will express itself interiorly, either somatically, in your body, or emotionally, in your psyche. One way or another, anger will make itself known.

Holding on to anger and other inner turmoil for the long haul overloads your healing system. What's your healing system? Our internal healing system has been called the most potent pharmacy that ever existed. The most important physical part of your healing system is your immune system. This intricate assemblage of parts, processes, and healing procedures responds to internal as well as outside forces. Sickness, even something as minor as a cold, can impede the immune system from functioning optimally. Other outside forces and stresses, such as stalled traffic, an inconsiderate supervisor, a marriage in need of some stimu-lation, a moment of anger with the kids, a grudge against your father, and so on, all impact the efficient operation of our immune system.

But how can we let go of anger and other inner turmoil? I would make three suggestions.

First, we have to separate the offense from the offender. We talked about this in our discussion of Key 6, "Forgive Others and Self." God calls us to love the offender and hate the offense, but too often we label somebody as being what their offense is. When the offender and the offense become identical in our mind, as if the two were one, we've got a potential problem. We must overcome the misperception that we are somehow lacking in justice when we forgive the deed. We will spiritually stumble over forgiveness if we believe we cannot forgive a person who has done some-thing wrong. There is never an injustice in looking past the misdeed to forgive the man or the woman. If we don't sepa-rate the offender from the offense, we can't follow God's call. Only God can forgive transgressions, but we *can* for-give our brothers and sisters, who as human beings are prone to make mistakes.

Second, we have to conquer fear. What fear? The fear that somehow the offender will perpetrate this transgres-sion again. Or the fear that if we forgive this offender, our entire value system will come crumbling down around our ears. Was Jesus afraid that the money changers would return to their jobs as soon as he left? Perhaps. Did he conquer his fear? It seems so. As I said before, he knew those money changers would return to the Temple, but he did not return to challenge them again. He forgave them, and his values did not crumble to dust at his feet. On the contrary, his forgiveness reinforced the value system that he was teaching his disciples.

Third, we have to work toward forgiving unconditionally. This means that we ask nothing from the man or woman we're forgiving. He or she need do nothing to deserve our forgiveness, neither apologize nor make amends nor even know. We forgive another person to free ourselves from the unhealthy grip of our own grudges. We are the primary benefactor of our love-action of forgiveness.

Again, here are the three ways to let go of anger and inner turmoil:

1. Separate the offender from the offense.
2. Conquer the fear of repeated transgressions.
3. Forgive unconditionally.

## Take Up the Business of Love

Anger and other emotional turmoil can serve as a vital mechanism of self-expression or as a disquieting conduit of discontent. Anger can bring internal conflict to a constructive conclusion, or it can rob us of peace of mind and throw us into a chaotic conflict. Anger itself is not the problem, but our way of expressing anger—or failing to express anger—can "throw a wrench" into our emotional works.

The people who age graciously—that is, with grace—and who do well in their senior years are people who have

allowed their anger to motivate them to get even closer to
people. They have harnessed their anger, gotten out of the
attack business, and taken up the business of love.

# Key 8

---

# Give of Yourself to Others

*For God is not unjust; he will not overlook your work
and the love that you showed for his sake in serving
the saints, as you still do. And we want each one of
you to show the same diligence so as to realize the full
assurance of hope to the very end.*

Hebrews 6:10–11

**Key 8 Definition:** The degree to which we actually
"do" for others in a selfless manner motivated by love.

## Giving Is Receiving

Jesus taught us so long ago that giving of self to help
others in need is actually a form of receiving (Acts 20:35).
From a worldly perspective this seems but a paradox. It
makes sense only when we see it through the eyes of Christ.
But behavioral scientists are now finding this apparent paradox to be true; further, they assert that helping others
appears to be good for our health as well and may even
extend our life. Soon our doctor may advise us to eat

nutritiously, exercise regularly, sleep restfully, "and give of yourself to others unselfishly" to achieve optimal health.

Is it any secret that those people who can give themselves away to others—not to the point of hurting themselves, but in a selfless way, motivated only by love—are the happiest people among us? For years the community of psychologists would not admit to the existence of altruism. *Altruism,* of course, means giving of oneself to another for no other reason than to help the other person. Psychology believed that the only reason we would help somebody else would be indirectly to help ourselves. If we were walking down the street and saw a homeless person in front of us, the only reason we'd give him a dollar, the community of psychologists would have said, would be to avoid feeling guilty. In a sense, so said the psychological community, we'd indirectly be helping ourselves by helping this homeless person.

I'm very pleased that the psychological community has reversed itself on this point and now believes that altruism is real. Behavioral science (or psychological) research has discovered that some pieces of human behavior don't fit into the previous conception of altruism. In other words, some people do things specifically, solely, and exclusively to help another person and not to help themselves. These people, who can give unconditionally to others, find great joy in living. Such people mature well and steadily grow in spiritual vitality and youthfulness.

Of course, the psychological community could not simply call this behavior *altruism.* They had to come up with a technically sounding name for it. What do you think they named altruism? Well, you might have guessed: *pro-social behavior.* Pro-social behavior means helping somebody else.

It's helping the culture and helping the people who are out there.

## Research Abounds

In the pages of the mental health–oriented journals, examples of the energizing effects of helping others abound. A large study done at the University of Michigan found that persons who regularly volunteered their time to help others heightened their overall zest for living and increased their life expectancy. Interestingly, researchers discovered that not all types of volunteering produced the same positive results; volunteering that brought people into close contact with others in need generated the most health-giving results for the volunteers. Volunteers who simply folded sheets or counted numbers did not benefit to nearly the same degree as volunteers who worked directly with needy people. The face-to-face encounter seems a powerful part of transforming "giving" into "receiving."

Stress researchers Maddi and Kobasa from the University of Illinois found that people who feel connected with others are calmer and less tense because of this connectedness. The notion takes on clarity when we remember that alienation makes us feel left out; it provokes fear, tension, and anxiety, all of which hasten the aging process. Could it be that giving of self in an altruistic fashion can actually slow down the aging process?

In a study at Harvard University led by psychologist David McClelland, investigators showed students a film of Mother Teresa doing good works among the poor of Calcutta. Blood samples taken from these students after they viewed the film contained higher levels of immunoglobulin A, an antibody that protects the body against infection. Blood samples from students who did not view the film showed no such increases. Evidently, even a brief and vicarious exposure to altruism has the power to shift our body's healing mechanisms in ways that enhance our constitutional hardiness and extend our longevity.

It's long been known that people with so-called Type-A personalities—hard-driving, hurried, and competitive—are statistically more prone to heart disease. More recent research points out that only certain Type-As are the most vulnerable for heart attack: those who show anger, irritability, and aggression as consistent behavioral traits. These folks are said to have an "angry heart." The well-known medical internist Dean Ornish, M.D., author of *Dr. Dean Ornish's Program for Reversing Heart Disease,* encourages his heart patients to do good things for others as an antidote to their unhealthy tendencies.

## Studies on the Aging Process

Studies searching for factors that influence the aging process have come to a similar conclusion; people who directly assist others in need, who can share themselves openly, are healthier and happier and live longer, more productive lives. The need for connection, for giving of self, seems to be a central ingredient in our internal health-promotion system. Somehow, it seems, soothing internal mechanisms, still not completely understood by modern science, become activated in a positive direction when we share ourselves with others.

Research on altruism, as reported in *Psychology Today* (October 1988), has found that we are more apt to help other people under certain conditions. We're more inclined to help someone if

1. We already know the person.
2. We see that person as being similar to us. The converse of this, of course, is that we are less apt to help a person whom we see as being different from us.
3. We live in a small town. Conversely, we're less apt to help other people if we live in an urban center. Since 85 percent of the American population lives in urban centers, we can deduce that there is much potential helping that is never made reality.
4. We feel as if there's no one else around to help. In other words, if it's just us and them, we will tend to get involved.

Flipping the coin over, we're less apt to help if

1. We fear appearing foolish. Fear seems to be the number one inhibiting factor. We do fear! If we fear that we'll look foolish, or if we fear that someone might say to us, "Why would you help them? They're just homeless; they need to help themselves," then we probably won't help. See how fear stops us from manifesting love on this plane?
2. We conclude that there's no need for help because other people aren't helping either. In other words, if a lot of other people are around, and no one seems to be helping, even if a person seems to be in need we probably won't help because no one else is helping.

You probably have read in the newspaper or heard on the radio about such cases. The most famous case occurred some years ago when more than two hundred people saw Kitty Genovese being murdered. The murder took place in broad daylight, and the murderer left his victim bleeding, but still quite alive, only to return to complete the heinous crime. No one even called the police.

3. We don't feel any personal obligation. We view the situation as the responsibility of someone else, or everyone else. We conclude that it's not my role to help. The government should do something to help this person. Or the Church. Or the Salvation Army. But not me.

## How We Feel When We Help

Some studies looking at "pro-social behavior" asked a very interesting question: How do we feel when we help someone? These studies came up with six different responses. The most common response was "I feel high when I help somebody else." In other words, people reported feeling good, feeling better about themselves. The second most common response was "I feel stronger and more energetic when I help someone." Third, "I feel warm all over"—a case of the "warm fuzzies." Fourth, "I feel calmer and less depressed when I help someone else." Fifth, "I feel better about myself. I have greater self-worth." Last, respondents said that they had fewer aches and pains when they helped somebody else.

Researchers took all this even further and asked, "How long does this feeling last when you help somebody?" Some people said it lasted just for the moment when they're actually doing the helping. This was a small minority. A greater percentage of the people said that it lasted all day. "When I help somebody in the morning it lasts all day. I feel good about myself all day." The vast majority of people said, "To feel good about myself all I have to do is remember what I did. When I remember what I did, I feel all of the great things I originally felt."

I'd like you to imagine something that may seem strange. Imagine that altruism could be made into a medicine, that we could convert helping others into an elixir...actually put it in the drugstore. Next, imagine that on the bottle it claimed that this medicine was guaranteed to make us feel euphoric, stronger, warm, calmer, and less depressed, to give us a feeling of greater self-worth, and to decrease our aches and pains. Finally, imagine that the instructions for taking the medicine said that we didn't have to take this medicine every day but only once, and that every time we even remembered that we had taken the medicine we would feel its effects all over again. Do you think the pharmacy would be able to keep this medicine on the shelf? The drug companies wouldn't be able to make enough of it!

We already have such a medicine. It's called helping somebody else.

When I was teaching resident doctors, instructing them on effective patient-physician interaction, I would recommend that the last thing they should put on the treatment regimen would be to go out and help somebody today. I think this is particularly true among patients who are retired. Some of them have worked helping people all their lives; when they retire, society seems to be telling them that they don't have to do that anymore, that all they need do is focus their energy on caring for themselves. For some more than for others, but for all to some degree, this self-focus leads to a personal devaluation, a stagnation of drive, and an anemia of enthusiasm. I'm overstating the case, perhaps; nonetheless, this may be the unwittingly damaging message they are getting.

Maybe that's the message that many of us get from or about retirement. If we ask anybody what the culture is saying about retirement, we'll hear something like "Well, I'm supposed to rest and mix my relaxation with playing." It's unfortunate our culture tells us something like, "Buy a big Winnebago and drive into the sunset" when we retire. Not that I have anything against rest or leisure, but resting, if that's all we do, will become for us the quickest path between here and the hospital. Even Martin Luther said, "When I rest, I rust."

The main function of rest or leisure is diversion. Did you ever go on a vacation and get to a place and say, "Ah, if only I could live in this place"? Some people actually do move to their former vacation spot, only to find that it has lost its luster. They sometimes find that this spot that formerly gave them so much diversion and play provides the same stresses and boredom they experienced at home.

Sometimes we have illusionary notions about what would be good for us. What makes a vacation good is the fact that we're not doing what we were doing the rest of the year. It is the very diversionary quality of the vacation that gives it the power to rejuvenate us, to refill us with energy and lots of other good things. It works much the same way with helping other people. Helping others diverts us from focusing egocentrically on ourselves.

Retirement is a good time to pursue such diversion. Instead of focusing on how much we need to rest, or instead of thinking about all the golf we can play or concerts we can attend or shopping we can undertake, we can apply this stage of our life to thinking about how we might be able to help those in need. Most retired people have more time and capability to help people than during their active working years. And altruism can provide a definite purpose to a life that our culture might regard as having outlived its usefulness.

## Love Operates beyond the Rules of the World

When we give of ourselves, what indeed are we giving? Giving can be disguised in innumerable forms, from understanding to empathy, from compassion to acts of service, and from tasks of altruism to any kind of doing good, but in whatever form giving to others takes, the core is still the same...giving of yourself is offering love.

The world teaches that when we give something away we have it no longer; we lose it. Love, as we know, operates beyond the rules of the world. Love is the only gift that multiplies the more we give it away. Jesus instructed us to multiply the gifts we have been given; the parable of the Talents (Matthew 25:14–30) is very clear on this point. For it is in giving that we can truly appreciate what we ourselves have been given. Further, if we do not give, we cannot receive (John 3:27). Conversely, when we hold onto the gifts we have received from God, we depreciate them, and we lose sight of who and what we are at our most essential level. We cut ourselves off from the healing channels connecting us with others.

In truth, unless we give our gifts away, we lose them. We

know this from other situations. If we have learned a second language but discontinue using it, we will soon lose it. Similarly, if we don't use our gifts—if we don't use the virtues that each of us has been given uniquely as gifts of the Spirit—we will lose them.

## Aging Requires We Rearrange Our Resources

Aging is a challenging state of life. Noted geriatrician Robert Butler, M.D., says that giving is stimulating, that meeting a challenge is invigorating. Aging is a challenging stage of life. The bodily strengths and capabilities upon which we formerly relied without a second thought no longer respond with the speed, agility, or grace they once did. Yet our resources do not disappear with age, they just need to be rearranged. Where once we had only strength, now we have determination; where once speed carried the day, now thoughtful understanding wins it; where once sensory sharpness gave us an edge, now patience and wisdom provide us with sustaining power.

But I would offer here an important word of caution. Whereas we are called to give of self to other people, we cannot honor God's children by dishonoring ourselves. I mean that it is very possible to lose sight of our own integrity in the process of giving ourselves away to other people.

Mother Teresa was probably the premier caregiver in our modern world. Do you think that when Mother Teresa put her head down on her pillow at the end of a long day of giving to other people, she beat her breast in remorse, bemoaning the fact she didn't get to minister to every person in Calcutta? I think not. I think that she probably thanked God for the strength and the gifts to do what she had needed to do that day. She wouldn't have decried what she couldn't do; instead, she would have thanked God for what she could do.

There are those among us whom we could label *co-dependent*. The term *co-dependent* refers to a persons who gradually gives her- or himself away in the service of someone else. A co-dependent person loses his or her self-definition in deference to the supposed needs of another. The co-dependent gives self away to such a degree that nothing of self is left, and becomes dependent upon the needs of the other. Co-dependents cannot even see that they are not really helping the other person, that they are merely perpetuating a cycle of dependency. We are not called to destroy ourselves. We are called to love, honor, and respect others, but not to the degree that we dishonor ourselves.

As Jesus gave of himself in his public ministry, he became, on his human level, more of a man, more of his human self. He "grew in grace and wisdom" throughout his entire earthly life. Yet he seemed to know when he needed to take leave of his healing and teaching ministry and seek his God in heaven; he needed to commune with God, to vacate the world and focus entirely on God. So too we need to give ourselves a rest from giving, however noble and loving our giving may be.

## What Are Retired Persons Supposed to Do?

At the core of our willingness to give of self lie our attitudes, values, and beliefs about our role and function on this earth. What is the fundamental purpose of our sojourn here? This question is perhaps nowhere more directly answered than by retirees who are free of the encumbrance of earning a living and who can devote their time, talents, and treasure to whatever they want. Some travel to all the places they have always wanted to visit. Some begin reading all the books they've always wanted to read. Still others spend as much time as they can with their children and grandchildren. Many others have found, perhaps after an initial period of self-indulgence, that they enjoy volunteering with the literacy program, or at the art museum or zoo, or for the crisis-pregnancy center or homeless shelter. All of these choices point to underlying values.

Goal-setting, or the lack of it, is perhaps the biggest obstacle. People fail to develop new roles for themselves when they cease performing the role of wage earner, homemaker, parent, spouse, or whatever else they have been doing for the previous thirty or forty years. In the absence of a productive role choice, these same retirees can lapse into the most passive and unproductive role in our culture, that of "patient." If people fail to develop an attitude of giving, they will instead retreat to a health-sapping mentality of entitlement and self-absorption. The same people who will admonish a younger person for not setting goals will act as if their own days of making decisions about life are over— as if now that they've retired they no longer need to learn or do or make plans about anything.

When life becomes simply a pursuit of aimless recreation pursued for its own sake, a person loses all awareness of others. Such a lifestyle will subtract from, not add to, health. It will sap the life out of even the most energetic person and may lead to sickness, aging, and premature dying.

Helping others appears to do the opposite; it strengthens and completes rather than weakens and fragments. Jesus commanded us to love one another and to give freely to one another: "You received without payment, give without payment" (Matthew 10:8). Spiritually vital people strive to give as Jesus gave, and in so doing they begin to live agelessly.

## A Wrapped Gift

The symbol for Key 8 is a beautifully wrapped present. Like a birthday or Christmas gift. Inside the box is a note card with one simple word: your name! Because we are the gift God is giving to the world. For us to withhold this gift means that we are constricting the flow of God's grace. We are called to be a conduit of God's love. To follow our calling, we give ourselves away. Not completely, for we always hold on to the integrity of ourselves—but we give our gifts away. In giving them away, we ensure that they are multiplied in us.

# Key 9

## Celebrate Your Faith

*Do not let your hearts be troubled. Believe in God, believe also in me. In my Father's house there are many dwelling places. If it were not so, would I have told you that I go to prepare a place for you?*

John 14:1–2

**Key 9 Definition:** The degree to which we develop an absolute personal assurance of the divine presence within us.

### Faith: A Central Ingredient of Youthfulness

Faith is, obviously, a central ingredient of our spiritual vitality, but not so obviously, faith is also a central ingredient in the development of youthfulness. Faith is our absolute assurance of the divine presence within, and it transforms the aging process into a real adventure of the soul. Faith protects us from despair, that state of despondency that can swallow us if we focus only on the physical level of our existence as we age. Those who live by faith cheat the dreaded thief of aging from stealing not only their youth but also their very self.

I've walked the halls of many nursing homes. I've also walked the campuses of many colleges. I can honestly say that often I've found more youthfulness in the nursing homes than in many colleges. Why? The faith manifested in nursing homes far surpasses the faith found on many college campuses. That faith is the cradle of the Spirit. It is that power within that inspires us to develop a personal relationship with God. True faith is more than a mere reverence for tradition; it is, rather, an all-encompassing personal conviction that quiets conflicting human desires, subdues spiritual doubts, and frees us from fear.

The gift of faith is the miraculous expectation of all things good. It allows us to stand patiently waiting for those "seeds" we have sown and tended in the garden of our soul to grow and bloom and produce abundantly.

Because of faith, we live with the resolute assurance that God's love within us is absolutely unassailable no matter what human adversity may attempt to violate it...even the adversities of aging. We have a penetrating understanding that more good than bad will come from whatever happens on this earthly plane. And we are certain that everlasting life awaits us after our inevitable physical death.

## Aging: Our Opportunity to Grow in Faith

Look what faith can do to transform the grief of physical decline into an adventure in spiritual empowerment. The world looks at aging as a senseless slippage into nothingness, a slow, almost tortuous, terrifying decline into disability, pain, and nonexistence. Faith silences the worldly-wise, assuring us that any suffering has a godly purpose and that death is only the horizon to the life beyond.

I remember being asked by one of our physicians to visit a patient in our hospital. I even remember the room number; it was room 339, on the third floor, and I knew the third floor to be the oncology floor. What I found in room 339 was a forty-nine-year-old teacher who had contracted the most virulent form of cancer known. When I walked into the room, I saw morose faces. As I leaned over the bed, I said to this patient, "I'm Dr. Johnson, and your doctor asked me to come up and talk with you." Her face contorted into a most hideous grimace and just exploded into tears, because I think she probably knew why I had been sent up. This formerly vibrant and vital woman "wasn't handling her cancer well."

She literally couldn't talk to me because of her tears, so I asked her husband if he would come out into the hall with me, and he did. With hands on his hips and a glare in his eyes that seemed somehow to hold me responsible for what was occurring in his wife's room, he said, "The doctors are giving her no hope, you know."

I knew that the doctors could do very little to forestall the aggressive growth of her cancer. I said, "This is such a tragedy that's going on here. How is your wife handling it?"

He retorted, "Well, they're giving her no hope, you know."

As I conversed more with him I realized I was talking to a man who had no faith. His wife apparently had no faith either. And I thought to myself, *Without faith, how could the doctors give you hope?* This man and his wife's hope was that the doctors could give them an experimental procedure, a one-in-ten-zillion chance, a shred of something that would somehow alleviate, however briefly, the thought that she was going to end forever. But the doctors had no procedure for keeping her body alive. She was certainly going to die. And without faith in God's eternal care, she was going to die afraid, alone, and in complete despair.

Dr. Bernie Siegel tells the story of a woman confronted by her physician. The physician told her, "We've brought everything that we possibly have to bring to bear onto your tumor. It's still growing. We can't seem to stop it. No radiology. No chemotherapy. We've given you everything we possibly can give you. If we give you any more chemotherapy it will completely obliterate your immune system and you'll be open to any kind of pathogen—any vector could come and attack you. We can't do anything more for you medically. The only thing you have is hope and a prayer."

The woman looked up at the doctor and asked, "Can you teach me how to hope and pray?"

These stories point out so clearly the necessity of faith. Faith plays a vital role not only at those tragic times in our lives when we are obviously being pressed to the wall, but also every day. What is it that allows us to get out of bed in the morning, to go to work or to school or perform all our activities of daily living, to put one foot in front of the other when we know that sooner or later we're going to reach the end of our earthly walk? If we didn't have faith, we would have no purpose for living. That's why faith is so important. Without it, we have no chance of feeling anything except despair.

## A Childlike Freshness and Happiness

Faith enables us to experience happiness. Christ told us that "unless you change and become like children, you will never enter the kingdom of heaven" (Matthew 18:3). As children have complete faith in their parents, so too we are to emulate this faith in our relationship with God. Trust in God allows us to put aside our worries, to forgive our fellow sisters and brothers, to focus on the present moment, to give ourselves to others, to seek love everywhere. None of the other keys to spiritual vitality is possible without faith. And when with faith we embrace these keys, we will find happiness there.

Without faith, aging becomes the dreaded tax collector, berating the limits on our time and treasure. Faith, however, reminds us that we have in us an inner sanctuary, a fortress of the infinite Spirit that is impervious to limitations or adversity. If you have faith, what is it that this world can take from us that is of any importance? It cannot take the most central treasure that we possess; it cannot take away our relationship with God. As Saint Paul assures us, "For I am convinced that neither death, nor life, nor angels, nor rulers, nor things present, nor things to come, nor powers, nor height, nor depth, nor anything else in all creation, will be able to separate us from the love of God in Christ Jesus our Lord" (Romans 8:38–39). This realization can tame all our doubts and quell all our conflicting human desires. It will free us from the fear of living and open our hearts to the possibility of loving.

## Faith and Mental Wellness

People exist in any one of four levels of mental well-being. The first level is *neurosis*. Neurosis stops us from living life to the fullest, and all of us are neurotic to some degree. For example, I don't like sharks. As a matter of fact, I could say I have a phobia about sharks. I love to go to the beach, but I won't go past that first sandbar because sharks live out there in the ocean. I've never invited a shark into my home, so I feel they probably don't want me in their home either. This is a neurosis that stops me from fully enjoying swimming in the sea. I also don't like high places, and this sometimes stops me from enjoying the view from high buildings and so on. These neuroses are relatively mild, and I can live my life quite well despite them. (Some phobias, however, are more severe and take people below the level of wellness into sickness.)

The next level of wellness is *sanity*. Men and women who are sane may go to work, cut their lawn, pay their taxes, and all that, but they are also people who have stopped growing. They seek security as their highest value, and their life revolves around avoiding problems. They don't seek opportunities for growth. They have difficulty grasping the true meaning of Christ's "Good News" and certainly don't consider aging as something to celebrate.

The next level is simply *wellness*. Being well means that you're doing everything possible on a human level to maintain your physical, emotional, and mental well-being. Well people exercise, eat well, drink alcohol in moderation (if at all), and get enough sleep. They educate themselves, develop friendships, and pursue activities with others. They do all they humanly can to actively promote their own wellness and well-being.

The highest level of well-being that we can attain on this plane is *spiritual awakening*. Notice, I'm not saying spiritually awaken*ed* because we're always in the process of waking up. "Waking up" means becoming more and more aware of the spiritual reality within us. When we are spiritually awakening, we are moving closer and closer to true reality, and thus closer to spiritual vitality and agelessness.

A common phrase we hear today is "Get real!" Normally, when someone tells you to "get real!" what he or she means is "get your head out of the clouds, get down to earth, can't you see how terrible things really are?" This is *not* what I mean by spiritual awakening. When people who are spiritually awakening "get real," they arrive at the point of seeing love wherever they gaze, for love is the true reality.

The highest level of well-being can also be called the level of *faith*. People who have reached this level have so much faith that when somebody says, "Get real!" they see this as a wake-up call to look for even more love—not less—in a particular situation. Faith enhances our power to love and be loved. It makes lovely for us anything that has the potential for loveliness. Anything that has the potential for loveliness, faith makes even lovelier. Isn't that a beautiful way to see the world?

## A Personal Time of Faith Action

How many times have you stepped out in faith? How many times have you said to yourself, "I don't know what the outcome is going to be, but I have faith that I'm supposed to be doing this." I remember a time in my life when my wife, Sandra, and I stepped out in faith. I had a very good job, we owned a modest yet comfortable home in a pleasant area, and we were putting money in the bank. We were doing all the "right" things, and we had two beautiful children at the time (eventually, we were blessed with a third). That should add up to the "good life." Yet amid this security and certainty, I began feeling strong "nudges" from the Holy Spirit to further my education by pursuing a doctorate.

I was teaching high school at that time and was head of my department, and I was very comfortable. So I questioned the internal nudges I was receiving. "What is this about wanting to go get a Ph.D.? What is this going to do to my life? I'd have to quit my job, sell the house, and take the kids to a faraway state." I was resisting the Spirit's promptings with everything that was in me. The funny thing is, the more I resisted, the more "pushed" I felt.

Together, we made the decision to step out in faith, without knowing what was actually going to happen. We packed the kids up in the Volkswagen and rode off. I will tell you that this decision—this stepping out in faith—not only opened up great chapters for me in my own personal and professional development, but led to much higher levels of happiness than I had ever experienced in my life. As Jesus teaches, "You know how to give good things to your children. How much more, then, will your Father in heaven give good things to those who ask him!" The Holy Spirit knew more about me than I did, and the only way for me to embrace that knowledge was to have faith that God was leading me to a better place, a place of God's choosing.

The way we greet our own aging is no different. We don't know what aging will bring, and we can't control it. The only way to be happy about it is to have faith that the Spirit has something to teach us and that God is leading us to a better place.

In my work, I'm struck so many times by the plans that adult children have for their aging parents. And I have to ask, "Whose plan do you think your parent will be following in their journey through the aging process?" If you have an aging parent, you can't delude yourself into thinking that it will be your plan that your aging parent will be using. It may not even be her or his plan, because most aging people in our culture have no plan. Some people do have a financial plan, but I can almost guarantee that almost everyone lacks a life plan for aging. It will be God's plan that will be worked out in their lives. To be open to God's plan, we've got to let go of our own plan and step out in faith.

Faith goes beyond belief. Belief is only intellectual, but belief can become faith when we translate it into loving action...when we act in faith. Indeed, we must have faith enough in faith to dare to take action.

## A Sailboat

The symbol for Key 9 is a sailboat. Faith is to our spirituality what sails are to a sailboat, not a burden but a means of movement. Faith brings power to us, and we are called to depend upon faith as our primary vehicle for spiritual development. We are called to have faith in faith. So hoist your sails as you head enthusiastically into the sunrise of what aging is and can be for you.

# Key 10

---

# Discover the Deep Meaning in Your Life

*I therefore, the prisoner in the Lord, beg you to lead a life worthy of the calling to which you have been called, with all humility and gentleness, with patience, bearing with one another in love, making every effort to maintain the unity of the Spirit in the bond of peace.*

Ephesians 4:1–3

**Key 10 Definition:** The degree to which we perceive an emerging state of God consciousness that energizes us to behold ever deeper levels of personal significance in our lives by earnestly devoting ourselves to God's purpose.

We suffer from a "meaning crisis" today. Consumerism has replaced altruism, commercialism has replaced mutuality, and the search for "more" has replaced our search for the good in ourselves and others. Body development has replaced character development. Litigation seems the "holy grail" of moral persuasion, while contentiousness, restlessness, and bluntness have overpowered harmony, peace, and justice. In such a chaotic and caustic world, it's no wonder we receive little support for developing an awareness of the deep meaning of life. And it's unfortunate because this awareness has the power to lead us down the most adventurous path to happiness, the kind of happiness that comes from living a life guided by the instructions outlined in the Beatitudes.

## Virtue Is Applied Love

Like happiness, we find "life-meaning" while pursuing something else. It is the by-product of devoting our life energy to serving God's purpose rather than our own. In short, we find life-meaning while pursuing virtue.

*Virtue* is best defined as "applied love." We practice virtue when we act in a loving manner. When we are kind, generous, patient, hopeful, charitable, trusting, faithful, accepting, empathic, and persevering, we are behaving virtuously. Practicing virtue provides us with marvelous opportunities to exercise and demonstrate the very faith we so much desire.

To apply love in our living, we must be awake. We must be alert to find God. One man who has helped awaken many people to the deep meaning of life is Victor Frankl. As you may know, Victor Frankl was a Jewish psychiatrist taken with his family to a Nazi concentration camp. While interred, he noticed that those people who had a sense of mission, a quest, a goal—what he called "a meaning in life"—seemed able to survive better in the camps than those who could discern no particular purpose for themselves.

This observation sent Frankl on a quest, and he devoted his whole professional life to understanding life-meaning. Indeed, he made the study of life-meaning his own meaning for life. He wrote a number of books and advanced a psychotherapeutic modality he called "logotherapy," all to help people find the deep meaning in their lives. His work, perhaps more than that of any other, has focused our attention on the mammoth value of life-meaning.

## Confusion about Life-Meaning

What is life-meaning? Meaning is actually an affective sensation—something that we feel internally, something that we experience affectively. If you have meaning in your life, you feel unique affective sensations. These sensations are much like those identified under Key 8, "Give of Yourself to Others": euphoria, strength, warmth, calmness, heightened self-esteem, and healthiness. This is not an exhaustive list, for each of us experiences the affective sensations of life-meaning differently.

But how do you get this sense of having meaning in your life? The only way to experience life-meaning is to have a life-purpose. When we have purpose, we cannot escape having meaning. If our life has no purpose, there's no way we can experience life-meaning.

And where does purpose come from? Life-purpose comes from a quest, a direction, a mission, a goal, an objective. Our life-purpose needs to be something bigger than ourselves, something that we may not ever completely achieve or master, yet something that we can adopt as the main directional thrust of our lives.

Knowing one's purpose seems simple enough when one

is going to school or raising children or designing bridges.
But the issue seems to become muddy for people who have
passed their so-called productive years. Our culture appears
decidedly confused about what exactly constitutes life-
meaning for mature adults who are retired. Their life stage
is often undervalued in our production-conscious world, and
the culture tells them that they are supposed to take care of
their body, rest, and have fun. Each of these three is necessary for everyone, but do these in and of themselves have
the power to bestow life-meaning? Are they not, rather, life-
sustaining activities that enable us to pursue a life-purpose
and develop life-meaning? If all that a person aspired to do
in life were exercise, rest, and have fun, that person, we
would have to conclude, would lack depth and purpose—
and, therefore, life-meaning.

So what is a person supposed to do during the retired
senior years? I would respond to this question very simply:
the corporal and spiritual works of mercy. To find meaning
in life—and not just during our retired years—we are called
to perform spiritual and corporal works of mercy.

| *Spiritual* | *Corporal* |
|---|---|
| Instructing | Feeding the hungry |
| Advising | Sheltering the homeless |
| Consoling | Clothing the naked |
| Comforting | Visiting the sick |
| Forgiving | Burying the dead |
| Bearing wrongs | Giving to the poor |

Our inspiration for performing spiritual and corporal
works of mercy comes from Jesus, who told us in the parable, "Truly, I tell you: just as you did it to one of the least

of these who are members of my family, you did it to me"
(Matthew 25:40). Feeding the hungry, satisfying the thirsty,
welcoming the outcast, clothing the naked, and visiting the
sick and imprisoned are the actions of love that will make
life meaningful.

## The Diamond

Love is an indefinable thing. The closest we can come to
defining it is to say that God is love and that God's works
are love. Love is the primary motive force of the universe;
we examined this as part of our discussion of the second
key to spiritual vitality, "Seek Love Everywhere."

Love itself may be too big, too strong, too overwhelm-
ing for us to see directly. Love is so brilliant that when we
stand in it's light we risk becoming blinded. Then how do
we see love? By its results, which we call virtues. Hope is
the result of love, and mercy, faith, charity, stamina, acceptance, simplicity, perseverance, humility...the list goes on.
True humility, for example, reveals love. We can't see the
love itself, just its action.

The diamond is the symbol of Key 10, "Discover the
Deep Meaning in Your Life." Imagine the diamond as representing ourselves. What do you as a diamond do to express love? Well, we know that a diamond is the hardest
substance on earth. Diamonds have many uses in industry,
but their primary function, or what we use them for the
most, is to reflect light. Did you ever look at a diamond in
the sunlight? It reflects all the colors of the rainbow, doesn't
it? A diamond flashes and sparkles like nothing else. It almost pulsates light out from itself. We can become stunned
or mesmerized by the beautiful brilliance of a diamond.

But let's stop and consider the nature of this light. What is it that's flashing at us? What is it that's reflecting the light? Is a diamond smooth? No, it has facets, many flat cuts on the surface, no matter what the diamond's shape—heart, pear, teardrop. It's not the diamond itself that reflects light. Light shines into the center of the diamond, is refracted by the stone, and is then reflected by one of the diamond's surfaces or facets.

If we conceive of the diamond as ourselves, then each of the facets can be seen as the actions that we undertake—that is, our virtues. Freely given by God through the Holy Spirit, the light of love shines into the heart of our diamond. This light is refracted by our acts of mercy and reflected throughout the world. As we gradually cut and polish the rough diamond that is us, we gradually increase our capacity to reflect God's love out to the world. And the more clearly and distinctly we can reflect God's light, the deeper the life-meaning we shall find in our lives.

Our maturing years can be thought of as God's gifts of time to us for the purpose of more finely cutting and polishing our diamond. In previous years we may have been somewhat distracted by the world from devoting the time and energy to diamond cutting and polishing. At times, we may have been so consumed by our day-to-day tasks that we completely forgot about the diamond. In our maturing years, we can readopt diamond cutting and polishing as our central lifework. The primary tasks of this work revolve around increased self-knowledge:

1. Analyzing the basic beliefs that direct the day-to-day operations of our life.
2. Clarifying our perception of the meaning of life.

3. Thinking from a faith standpoint.
4. Feeling with the heart of Jesus.
5. Developing greater powers of discernment so that we can respond rather than simply react.
6. Acting with the strength, conviction, and humility of God.

## Basis for Character Development

It's interesting to note that the word *virtue* appears only three times in the New Testament: Mark 5:30, Luke 6:19, and Luke 8:46, where it is used to describe the healing power of Christ. Indeed, in the Revised Standard Version of the Bible, the word *power* is substituted for *virtue.* Remember the story of the woman with the hemorrhage, and how she touched the hem of Jesus' garment? The newer translations quote Christ as saying, "I can feel the power draining from me." Older translations read, "I can feel the virtue draining from me." Virtue gives power, the power to be what we truly are, children of God rather than children of the world.

While virtue is mentioned only three times by name, specific virtues such as faith, mercy, hope, trust, acceptance, charity, forbearance, and many others are mentioned over and over again. The necessity for virtue development seems unassailable in both the Old and the New Testaments. As the Scriptures seem to point out, the virtues provide an unshakable foundation for our spiritual growth. And the tireless inner voice of the Spirit is constantly nudging us toward virtue development.

There is good reason for this. Our personal virtue development will enable us to accept the inevitable physical losses we will experience as we age. Simultaneously, our experience of loss will strengthen the virtues within us. To replace our losses on the physical plane, we adopt virtues even more solidly than we did yesterday. Indeed, we could say that loss is the primary force for virtue because it provides the opportunity for love to move into our life. What process but aging could teach the virtue of patience so thoroughly, or adaptability with such force, or forbearance so tangibly, or wisdom in such depth? In the rich classroom of aging we can most effectively learn the path to God.

Furthermore, growth in one virtue leads to the development of others. For example, as you grow in the virtue of strength, the virtue of self-discipline naturally follows. As hope advances, so does peace. As humor enriches the soul, humility, transcendence, and kindness move in as well.

Interestingly, if you could learn any virtue perfectly—which, of course, no human being can—you would have learned them all. Because they're all interconnected and they all have the same source. That source is God's love.

## Virtue Is More Than Its Own Reward

Being virtuous, however, is not a popular concept in today's culture. Despite the popularity of *The Book of Virtues,* by former Secretary of Education William Bennett, our media seem to do all they can to avoid the term entirely, evidently for fear of being "out of step with the times," "untrendy," or, worse yet, "prudish." When was the last time you saw a sitcom that used applied virtue as the unifying theme in its weekly plot? This attitude is not hard to understand. The popular media speak for the world, and virtue clearly originates from grace, a force quite beyond this plane. Unfortunately, the worldly-wise think that virtuous people aren't sexy and, of course, don't like anything that isn't sexy.

More than that, the worldly-wise perceive no reward for being virtuous and so deride virtue as being its own reward. And it's true that virtue is seldom rewarded by the world. God, however, rewards virtue far beyond any prize the world could ever bestow, giving the kingdom of God now to those who act virtuously. And one of the gifts of the kingdom, I would repeat, is the gift of youthfulness.

What does this have to do with life-meaning? Another of the rewards of virtue development is an energizing awareness of God as active in our life. Seeing the love of God changing the world through our own works of mercy cannot but emphasize the meaningfulness of our own lives.

## Ultimate Failure of Life

Dr. Bernie Siegel explains that dying is not our ultimate failure. Rather, a person's ultimate failure would be the refusal to take on the challenges of life. There is no life stage more challenging than the life stage of senior living because we are beset with life losses that can either embitter us or empower us. The choice is ours. These losses create a vacuum, into which we can inject either fear or love. If we fill the vacuum with fear, we will harvest the fruits of fear: vice. But if we fill that vacuum with love, we'll reap the fruits of love: virtue. People who fill the vacuum of loss with fear will end up either cantankerous or depressed. But those who fill the vacuum of losses with love will be hopeful, charitable, and faith-filled.

Is it easy to choose love? No. Growth is hard and sometimes painful, and we can encounter all kinds of road barriers along the way. But I'm reminded of something my favorite psychologist, Abraham Maslow, said: "As we travel the path of life and we come to a fork in the road, take the most risky path because therein lies the most growth."

I believe that we are supposed to enter into the aging process knowing it is a risk and embracing the riskiness of it. And I believe that the virtues we have developed in getting to this point will help us continue to grow throughout our maturing years. For this reason, it's important to polish the facets of our diamond at every stage of life, so that when we do move into the later phases we will already have the ability to step out in faith, motivate in hope, find peace, and reflect God's love in the unique way that God has planned for us.

# Key 11

---

# Make Your Feelings Work for You

*"Now my soul is troubled. And what should I say—*
*'Father, save me from this hour'? No, it is for this*
*reason that I have come to this hour."*

John 12:27

**Key 11 Definition:** The degree to which we can manage the emotional reactions to the events of our lives, our relationships, and the sum total of the circumstances within which we find ourselves as we mature.

We have feelings about everything, don't we? Feelings are visceral responses to thoughts. The thoughts that we put in our minds are evaluations; they are the judgments that we make about any incident, relationship, or event that crosses our mental horizon. Our thoughts are the meaning that we discern from the circumstances of our lives. Our feelings are simply our emotional reactions to those thoughts.

Some feelings refresh the soul, inspire the mind, and re-
new the spirit, while others diminish the heart through discouragement and disappointment. We are not, however,
trapped into feeling any particular way. Part of growing
wiser as we grow ever more mature is learning that we can
choose which kind of feelings we allow to linger within.

Of all the functions of the personality, feelings are the
most difficult for us to accept. Feelings pose the most direct pain potential of any of the functions; this is precisely
because we *feel* them. We may not know what we're thinking, but many times we have at least a vague sense of what
we're feeling, even if it's only "good" or "bad."

Sometimes people are completely unable to express their
feelings. Psychiatry calls such people *alexithymic*. Literally, *alexithymia* means having no words for feelings. When
asked, "How are you feeling?" an alexithymic person will
say, after a very long pause, "OK" or "good" or "no good."
Such people are not facile in expressing their feelings because they are blocked in connecting a felt sense with a
word. Unfortunately, each of us is alexithymic to some degree, unable to express how we feel, and hence unable to
feel.

## A Stage

The symbol for Key 11 is a theatrical stage. Feelings are
the movers of the drama of our lives. When we are feeling,
we are participating in all that is going on around and within.
We are connected to the events of life and to the other char-
acters in it. If we aren't feeling, however, we experience no
drama, we are flat, we are blunted. We are failing in some
critical way to experience what life is all about. Without

wonder, awe, delight, and motivation, life becomes just a monotonous succession of detached events. The topography of a life without emotion would resemble a desert, awe-inspiring at first, perhaps, but then endlessly flat and empty. Every place on this earth has it's beauty, yet a life without feelings becomes a stage where beauty is hard to find.

To understand our feelings, we must be able to put words to our visceral sensations. When we can express our feelings in words, we come closest to genuinely living the marvelously interesting drama of life. This self-expression requires that we learn how to *respond* to our feelings, not simply *react* to them. This is a difficult but important distinction to understand.

People who react to life let forces outside themselves make life decisions for them. On the other hand, people who respond to life generally look into themselves for the "answers." They discern their own beliefs, their own perceptions, their own thinking, and their own feelings. They put all these data together with what they "hear" from their omnipresent internal teacher, the Holy Spirit, and come up with a course of action that is well considered on all levels of their existence: body, mind, and spirit.

Many of us have never learned this difference because we were raised in alexithymic families. I include myself in this category, since I was raised in a family that really didn't know how to deal with feelings. When a family refuses to give credence to feelings, the children receive the message that feelings will not be honored, nor will they be discussed. Admonitions like "Well, you shouldn't feel that way" or "Why would you feel like that?" are basically saying, "We would rather not hear from you about your feelings." A family with such attitudes about feelings is a family that finds itself living offstage, so to speak, and missing the central drama of their lives.

Why are so many families like this? Because feelings can be very fearsome. The central fear is that if feelings come out, somebody gets hurt. So children often learn, "If you're not going to say anything good, don't say anything at all!" That may sometimes be a good rule, but if it prevents you from showing any of your feelings, what are you doing to yourself? If you're so afraid of feeling that you strangulate all of your emotions, you'll never be able to take your rightful place on the stage of your life.

## Feelings Always Find Expression

Our feelings will always find expression. A spiritually healthy person will be able to express his or her feelings in an appropriate and targeted way. A spiritually unhealthy, alexithymic person, on the other hand, will not be capable of external emotional expression, so his or her feelings break out internally.

What is the number one way of ensuring that we don't express our feelings? We "stuff them." We "push them under the rug" or "shove them down the pipe." Some of us even put a nice "gloppy" cap on these feelings so they're sure to stay down, burying them beneath mounds of ice cream or layers of pizza.

And what happens to these feelings when we stuff them down the pipe? Do you think there's a nice little vessel down there, something like your spleen, that collects and then eliminates all our stored-up feelings? We use the expression "venting our spleen" to indicate when we're letting all those stored-up feelings come exploding out, but "venting our spleen" is simply an inappropriate way of releasing the pressure from too many stuffed-down feelings. There is no emotional "storage and elimination" chamber in our psyches.

Rather, when we "stuff" our feelings, we send them into our joints, our lungs, our bowels, our heads, our necks, our shoulders, our lower backs, our stomachs, our hearts. When we do this over and over again, we make our bodies sick.

I have a dear friend who is a dramatic example of stuffing feelings. A really wonderful woman who's been married for more than forty-five years, she suffers from osteoporosis, an erosion of the bones of her body. This erosion takes place mainly in her neck and her spine and is very painful. The pain is not constant but irregular, coming in waves that may last two or three days, during which she is forced to take to her bed. Sometimes she's even driven to her physician, who treats her with cortisone injections to dull the excruciating pain.

For years this woman has held grievances against her husband, for his selfishness, vanity, nonempathy, and so on. Yet only rarely has she confided her intense feelings about her husband to anyone; she prefers to stuff them. You know, of course, where she is stuffing her feelings: in her bones and joints. Figuratively, she regards her husband as a big pain in the neck, a load to be carried around, an emotional burden for her at the very least. Her perceptions become critical thoughts, and these lead to feelings that are just too intense and alien for my friend to assimilate or communicate. She believes that a loyal wife shouldn't express negative feelings about her husband, and she's also afraid of the feelings that she has toward her husband. She doesn't believe in divorce, but she doesn't know how to deal with this man. So her stuffed feelings find their favorite targets in her spinal column.

Another psychological trick we perform with our feelings is to displace them. *Displacement* means that we take our feelings out on something else. This is sometimes called the "kick the dog" reaction. If we're upset about an unsuccessful shopping trip or angry about a friend's slight, we displace these unwanted feelings by shoving the dishes around in the sink, yelling at the cat, slamming the door, neglecting the house, and so on. Displacement is a way of expressing feelings without having to deal with anyone. The problem with displacement is that it doesn't do the job; in the long run, we're still stuck with our feelings.

Yet another unfortunate thing we do with our feelings is to project them. What does *projection* mean? Let's look at an example. Let's say that your sister in California upsets you. Instead of responding directly to her in some way, you may project your feelings of anger at your spouse, your best friend, or your children. You may take your negative feelings toward your congresswoman and emotionally hurl them at your neighbor. You may take your frustrations at a store clerk's insensitivity and project them at your priest or minister. In work situations this is known as "passing the buck." The big boss reprimands a supervisor, the supervisor in turn chastises the foreman, the foreman takes out her anger on the shift supervisor, and so on until the entire working environment has become toxic.

What normally happens when we project our feelings onto somebody else is that they come back a hundredfold. My mother, a woman of many and frequent sayings, would remind me often, "Richard, spread crumbs on the water and they come back to you a hundredfold." The adage works the same whether the crumbs are positive or negative feelings.

Another psychological trick we have for dealing with our feelings is called *reaction formation*. Let's say that you are dissatisfied with your spouse for some reason. Instead of confronting him or her with your raw feelings, you turn them around. You smother the person with compliments, projecting positive feelings onto him or her while actually meaning just the opposite. Within the positive feelings we project is embedded a long list of expectations about what we want our spouse to do, or be, or say, or get. In my practice I see many marriages that are not primarily love relationships but what I call "special relationships." A special relationship is one in which each party believes that the other "has an obligation to satisfy me. If you don't meet these expectations, what am I going to be left to think about you? You're not measuring up. I can only keep feeling positively toward you as long as you keep meeting my needs." Special relationships emerge when the couple is not emotionally honest with each other.

## How We Deal with Feelings

Are there any positive ways to deal with feelings? I'm going to assert something that sounds simplistic here, but I want to make sure that it comes through clearly. What are we supposed to do with our feelings? *Feel them!* We're supposed to feel our feelings. Every writer, every researcher, every psychologist who has studied our emotions has come to the very same conclusion.

What does this mean? Does it mean that we're supposed to walk around all day with a long morose face on because it's going to cost two hundred dollars to replace the wind-shield on your car? Are we supposed to bounce off the walls all day because we're waiting to hear if our mortgage was approved? That's not really what I mean by feeling your feelings.

Alcoholics Anonymous (AA) has a rhyming guide that reminds people how to deal with feelings. The five steps to dealing with feelings are to

1. Name them
2. Claim them
3. Tame them
4. Aim them
5. Exclaim them

### Name Your Feelings

We may have a multitude of feelings at any given moment of our lives. If we are to manage them productively, we first need to identify what our feelings are, especially those that might be causing us a problem. The first step in con-structively managing your feelings is to determine what indeed you are feeling right now. This fundamental step is not as elementary as it might appear. It entails assessing your emotional state and then choosing the appropriate word or words that describe your feelings as accurately as pos-sible. It might be easy, for example, to say, "Well, I'm feel-ing angry," and perhaps you are. But you might also be feeling hurt, rejected, spurned, insulted, maligned, reviled, or any number of additional emotions. It's important to rec-ognize the layers of interconnected feelings and to identify all of them. Only then will you be able to deal with each one.

### Claim Your Feelings

The next step is to "own" our own feelings, to admit that these feelings belong to us and to no one else. We must say, "*I* am sad...despondent...discouraged...downcast for this moment." This is an extremely important step because many people have prohibited themselves from feeling certain emotions. For example, many people do not allow themselves to feel happy or joyful. So they are unable to "own" feelings of happiness when they occur; they are unable to say, "*I* am feeling cheerful...joyous...mirthful now."

Feelings are like big waves. If you're playing in the surf and notice a huge wave coming, you might say, "Oh boy, that wave is enormous; it's going to overwhelm me." You may try to fight it: "No wave is going to push me around; I'm going to stand my ground." But this is not going to work, because the wave is way too big. So you try to outrun it: "Gangway! I'm getting out of the water." But the wave is coming much too fast. You might try to swallow it: "I'm bigger than you, Wave." No, it's much bigger than you are. Maybe you'll dive into it: "Watch out, Wave; coming through." You may fare better by this action, but you're still not going to get very far. The only way to deal with a huge wave coming at you is to become a part of it: "*I* am Wave for this short moment." Interestingly enough, riding a wave is the only way to get over it. And "owning" or feeling your feelings is the only way to get beyond them too.

It's also important to realize that neither Tom, nor Sue, nor Dr. Bill, nor Fr. John, nor Mom made you feel exuberant...gloomy...irritable. These are your feelings, not theirs. It's not like catching a cold; you didn't get your feelings from someone else, they arose within you. You created them, and you can't give them away either. They belong to you alone.

### Tame Your Feelings

Since feelings come from within, the third step is to tame or control them. To do this, figure out what thought or thoughts served as the catalyst for a particular feeling. How did you "talk" to yourself internally? "What did I say to myself that caused me to feel shame...trepidation...optimism?" Once you've clarified what thoughts generated the feeling, the next question is whether this thinking is reasonable and logical. At this point, change is possible. Not a single person is commanded to think in any particular way; you can think whatever you like. So why would you continue to think irrationally? In ways that cause pain? You don't have to; you can change the way you're thinking right now.

You can adopt the mind of Christ and think as he would. Whenever you become perplexed, you can ask, "Is this what Jesus would want me to think right now?" How many times in the gospels does Jesus advise us, even command us, to choose love and to reject fear? "Take heart, it is I; do not be afraid" (Matthew 14:27, Mark 6:50); "Do not fear those who kill the body" (Luke 12:4); "But he said to them...do not be afraid" (John 6:20); "Do not be afraid, but speak..." (Acts 18:9)? Over and over again Jesus instructs us to move away from feelings of fear and toward feelings of love. He even tells us to love our enemies: "Love your enemies and pray for those who persecute you" (Matthew 5:44). Because Jesus would not tell us to do something humanly impossible, we know that it is possible to alter the way we feel by changing the way we think. When we examine our thoughts in this way, we can begin to take control of them, and thus to tame our feelings.

### Aim Your Feelings

The point of the "aim" step is to generate options for expressing a particular feeling. Remember, feelings will find expression. The question is whether you want to aim the feeling or allow it to somehow find its own expression and target?

In addition to advising us about what to feel, Jesus also demonstrates for us the different options available for expressing feelings. The parable of the Good Samaritan (Luke 10:25–37) is about giving options for behavior based on feelings. Remember, the Samaritan, unlike the priest and the Levite, was moved with pity. Here is a clear example that Jesus gives us about how we are to deal with feelings. On another occasion (Luke 12:22–31), Jesus warns his disciples not to fall prey to the feeling of worry (anxiety) about earthly issues such as food and clothing; rather, he encourages them, focus on how God provides for you. These are clear directions for the healthy management of our feelings. Recognizing that we do indeed have choices is central to Christ's message of love to us.

So you ask yourself, "What are my options in expressing this feeling? Where and in what are the healthiest ways for me to express this emotion?" You may come up with a short list, which leads you to the next step.

To aim your feelings means coming up with alternative ways of expressing them; you're just "brainstorming" possibilities at this point. Jean feels sad that neither of her adult sons seems to show an interest in her. She pines for them, for their calls, for their contact. Jean is a self-effacing person who finds asking for things for herself very difficult. Together we generated some options for expressing her sadness and her underlying feelings of anger. She could

- call each of them and invite them over
- talk to their wives with the same request
- write each son a letter describing her thoughts and feelings
- request a counselor to effect a family meeting
- pray that the emotional estrangement will end
- do nothing at all

This list is only representative; you could undoubtedly expand upon it. The point here is that it is from among this array of alternatives that Jean will choose what to do and then move on to the next step.

### Exclaim Your Feelings

Once we have generated several options, you now choose one alternative as the best course of action. Then, you actually take action. You express your feeling in the way that you have decided is healthiest for you.

It's important to remember that expressing your feelings does not give you license to hurt someone. We have a *mandate* to express feelings, but not in ways that will hurt people. All we're trying to do is exclaim them accurately and get beyond the wave.

One note: Deciding not to express a feeling outwardly *is* a constructive form of expression. If you have moved with diligence through the first four steps, only to decide that expressing this feeling outwardly would be imprudent, then your decision not to demonstrate the feeling can, on occasion, be considered constructive.

## Feelings Ask Us to Make Decisions

There's an old Midwestern adage that goes, "Son, you don't have a problem, you've got a decision to make." The main function of feelings is to motivate us to make decisions. Let's see how this is supposed to work.

The personality has six functions, as follows:

1. To believe
2. To perceive
3. To think
4. To feel
5. To decide
6. To do or to act

A person who is functioning healthily will move through these steps, arriving at a decision and embarking on a course of action. However, many people get caught in what I call the "three-four rut." Their thinking causes them to feel a certain way, but they cannot act on their feelings. And when people don't move from feeling to decision making, they may experience depression.

Let's look at an example. You believe, "All auto mechanics should be honest." That's your thought. However, let's say that you just ran into an auto mechanic who isn't honest—you've perceived she's been dishonest with you. (I'm not trying to disparage auto mechanics; this is simply an example.) You then think, "She's not an honest mechanic," and you continue, "Since she must be a dishonest person, she must be a bad person." Do you hear the evaluation there? What kind of feeling will you have as a consequence of that evaluation? Anger? Mistrust? Fear? You could, as a result, decide, "I'll take my business someplace else" or "I'm going to small-claims court" or, at least, "I'm going to give her a piece of my mind." Even a decision not to do something is a decision, perhaps a good one, as long as you admit and "own" your feelings about the situation. Instead, you go back to the third function of the personality, thinking, and begin the cycle all over again: "Not only is she a dishonest mechanic, she's the worst mechanic I've ever seen in my life." What happens to your feelings? Your anger/mistrust/fear intensify. Then instead of moving on and making a decision, you go back yet again and think, "Not only is she the worst mechanic, but this is the worst shop in the world, and her boss is probably no good either." You are neither evaluating the accuracy of your thinking nor expressing your feelings constructively. Indeed, you may not even be aware that you are in a three-four rut. So you won't know why you're getting more and more frustrated, why you end up stuck with your feelings of anger or mistrust or fear. You haven't managed your feelings; on the contrary, you've allowed your feelings to manage you!

Unfortunately, when people get stuck in the three-four rut, they usually end up depressed. They believe that they can deal with their feelings by thinking their way out of them, but when thinking only seems to intensify their feelings, they get extremely frustrated. If their thinking continues to get them nowhere, they get depressed.

## Depression

Depression is a serious sickness, and mature adults suffer with it at disproportionally higher rates than any other age group in our culture. Actually, there are many depressions. Some depression is strictly biological. We can treat biological depression medically; our discussion will not deal with this sort. Let's briefly discuss those other depressions that are not exclusively biologically rooted.

Depressions often stem from our inability to deal with our feelings more adroitly. When patients come into my office, one of the things we try to do is clarify or "get in touch" with their feelings. As we said above, people need to "own" their feelings; they need to say, believe, and know, "These are *my* feelings." This step is mandatory before decision making is possible. In truth, the only thing that will help someone move beyond most depressions is to begin making decisions. Even most of what we call client-centered, or Rogerian, therapy, which starts with feelings, must eventually culminate in some sort of action.

When I counsel mature adults, I try to move them away from the debilitating evaluations that they make in step three and toward taking action in step six. Anyone who participates in counseling needs to be aware that counseling is not simply holding a hand and listening to feelings. The counselor wants something to happen. When my clients are open to change and willing to make their feelings work for them, wonderful things can happen.

## Final Note

Make no mistake about it, life is a drama, and you're on stage every day of your life. Shakespeare was right when he talked about the world as a stage. I have a senior-adult friend who conceives of his life as a movie in which he is the main character. He lives a colorful life, filled with love and vitality.

Christ called us to live this life well and live it to the fullest, not to put our light under a bushel basket, but to put it on a pedestal.

And I would add, "Put your pedestal on a stage."

# Key 12

---

# Achieve Balance in Your Life

*[God] has made known to us the mystery of his will, according to his good pleasure that he set forth in Christ, as a plan for the fullness of time, to gather up all things in him, things in heaven and things on earth.*

Ephesians 1:9–10

**Key 12 Definition:** The degree to which we can bring the various arenas of our lives into a harmonious integration; a condition of life in which we give equalizing energy to each arena of our lives.

Enlightened healthcare professionals have long espoused the concept of life balance—the harmonious integration of all arenas of life—as the fulcrum for overall wellbeing. Even the ancient Greeks preached a variation of the notion, advocating the development of a "sound mind and a sound body" as pivotal to health and happiness. Jesus brings completeness to the concept when he teaches, "Give

153

therefore to the emperor the things that are the emperor's,
and to God the things that are God's" (Matthew 22:21,
Mark 12:17, Luke 20:25).

## The Wisdom inside Us

The whole process of maturation occurs quite naturally and
imperceptibly, so much so that we may not even be conscious of it. Not until some startling event bursts into our
lives do we usually become aware that some primary shift
has taken place within us, a shift that alters our former attitude in some fundamental way. The experiences we have
encountered to date have stored up valuable lessons in our
internal treasure chest, and we can retrieve these lessons to
meet this new developmental challenge with more stamina
than even we thought we possessed. Upon the birth of a
child, the death of a parent, the loss of a job, the experience
of bodily injury or sickness, we are forced to dig deeply
into our storehouse of learning, adjustment, and coping.
Aging is another such turning point in our life, albeit a more
gradual one.

Aging is often misunderstood because what is generally
regarded as aging are simply the natural changes that occur
over time to physical objects of any sort. Wood rots, metal
rusts, rock crumbles, and soil erodes. As all physical material is constantly changing, so is our body. Yet what is commonly seen as aging on the physical level is more accurately
seen as maturation on the mental level and as enlighten-
ment on the spiritual level. The body ages; it goes the way
of all flesh and all physical matter. Its nature is to disintegrate. The nature of the mind is to become more aware, to
think more accurately, to awaken progressively. Likewise,

the spiritual core of us accumulates experience and, with the assistance of the Holy Spirit working in conjunction with an awakening mind, generates that quality of life mastery we call wisdom. We are essentially spiritual beings, made conscious by our ability to think, to feel, to decide, and to act, all placed in an energy package we call our bodies.

## A Spinning Top

The symbol for Key 12 is a spinning top. More precisely, a particular type of spinning top: a plate spinning on top of a shaft, such as you may have seen at a circus. The plate and the shaft, of course, are separate, detachable, but when the plate is in balance, the circus clown needs to do very little to keep it spinning. I think of that plate as representing your life. When your life is in balance it takes very little energy to keep it going, to keep the "plate" of your life running efficiently and effectively. However, what happens when things get out of balance? Let's take some mashed potatoes, for example, and put them on the edge of the plate. What happens? It starts wobbling, and the clown needs to pay that much more attention to keeping the plate going and spinning. In the same way, we will begin wobbling if we live an unbalanced life, and just keeping on will require a tremendous amount of energy, leaving us less energy for enjoying life.

## What Is Life Balance?

Balance, or lack of it, spells the difference between living a life of calm or turmoil, pain or pleasure, God-consciousness or world-consciousness. People who can balance their lives are those who have spiritual vitality, who discover the agelessness that resides within them. So the question is, *How do we balance our lives?* To know this, we must understand what we need to balance.

Let's look to the circus again: Have you ever felt as if your life is a circus? Life is like a circus, but instead of having three rings, it has six. You may be reminded of the six functions of the personality, but this is different. The six-ring circus that is your life can be divided into what I prefer to call the *Six Arenas*:

1. Career or Ministry Life
2. Family or Community Life
3. Relationships Life
4. Self Life
5. Faith Life
6. Leisure or Fun Life

These six come in no particular order; each one of us arranges our life just a bit differently. The order—perhaps *priority* is a better word—depends on how much energy we invest in each arena of life at any given time. We have only a certain amount of life energy available; how we allocate it determines what our priorities are.

Everything you undertake belongs in one or more of these six life arenas. Think of what you're doing right now: you're reading this book. In which of the six life arenas are you most centrally investing your energy at this moment? Most probably, number four: the self life. Perhaps some of your energy is also being invested in the faith life arena. Because this is a faith-driven, self-help book as well as a spiritual development book, we could assume that these two arenas would be paramount. It's common to see overlapping between two life arenas in any particular endeavor.

By the way, the self life arena has two aspects to it. First, "self life" refers to your relationship with your "self," your soul; second, it involves your relationship with your body. Did you know that you have a relationship with everything in your body? Every limb, organ, nail, hair, and so on.

When a person lives an unbalanced life, he or she is putting a disproportionate amount of their life energy into one or several of these six life arenas. Overloading one life arena renders the other life arenas anemic or poverty stricken. The most common example is to look at the so-called workaholic. He or she concentrates almost exclusively on the career life arena, leaving no time or energy to enjoy any other arena. Here is a graphic image of an unbalanced life.

What *is* life energy, anyway? The most effective way to describe life energy is simply to say that each of us has 100 percent of life energy at all times. Even though we think we don't always have it all, we do. And we're always "robbing Peter to pay Paul." If we want to put more energy into our leisure arena, for example, we've got to take it from someplace else. We get into problems when we think we can burn the candle at both ends. Try putting 120 percent of energy into one arena and see how quickly you burn out. So the operative question is, *What portion of this 100 percent are we allocating to each of the six life arenas at any given time?*

## Life Balance and Sickness

I've already mentioned that I formerly taught medical residents in a hospital setting. These residents were one, two, or three years out of medical school. How much of their life energy do you think they were putting into the arena of career life? Upward of 90 percent. Faculty members almost expect medical residents in their first year (better known as the internship year) to become depressed at some point. These residents are living such an unbalanced life that the strain of the imbalance places them at risk for depression. The same is true for all of us; when we live an unbalanced life, giving ourselves little respite or diversion, we fall prey to all sorts of maladies.

Whenever our lives are "out of kilter," we will get sick. It's not "you might get sick" or "perhaps you'll get sick," it's "you will get sick." It's a matter of when, not if; a matter of severity and location too: what part of our body or mind will it strike, and how severe will it be. We can't know the answers to those questions in advance.

Our goal, then, is to try to smooth out our life, to try to bring balance to it in some way. This does not mean that we need to put exactly the same percentage of energy into every life arena. In truth, as we move through the developmental phases over the life span, we will know times when we are called to put more energy in one arena or another. But as we move into the later phases of life, we have a golden opportunity to really smooth out, or equalize, or reallocate our life energy among the six life arenas. We have the freedom to create life balance that was heretofore impossible.

Some mature adults might say, "But why would I need a career life arena? I'm retired." This question seems logical on the surface, but upon closer scrutiny it shows the seeds of a very dismal retirement life. I gave a televised interview on retirement living some time ago. When I arrived at the TV studio, the station manager greeted me at the door with the statement, "Gee, you've got to meet Ray. Ray's one of our cameramen, and he's been here since the day the station opened, but next week he's retiring."

So I went to see Ray. And right after I said, "Ray, nice to see you," I asked, "What are your plans for retirement?"

He responded without hesitation: "I'm going fishing."

I knew then that he would have problems. Ray thought he could balance his life simply by taking care of himself and having what he thought was the best fun in the world. Now, I've nothing against fishing. I'm glad people fish. I've even done it a few times myself, but I always wished I didn't catch any of the critters. Most of the fishing I did was with my own children, and I spent most of my time putting worms on hooks and untangling lines anyway. That's OK. We still had fun. But Ray was headed for a retirement disaster! The problem was that he thought he was going fishing for the rest of his life. What he was telling me was, basically, "I'm going to have a great retirement by living this wonderfully unbalanced life." Ray didn't realize that he was going fishing in a leaking boat, so to speak, and that if he didn't fix the boat—if he didn't pay attention to all of life's arenas— his fishing trip was going to be a short one. If all he did with his retired years was go fishing, he would soon find himself sinking into debilitating apathy and sickness.

Like everyone else, Ray could not possibly live a balanced life with his current retirement plan; he needed a much more robust life plan for his retirement years, one that included focusing on all of life's arenas, including his "career."

What is the "career" of a retiree who no longer has a job every day? What about the quest, the mission, the purpose?

Isn't this what the tenth key to spiritual vitality is all about: "Discover the Deep Meaning in Your Life?" If you don't have a quest, or a purpose, then something's out of balance in your life, and you cannot be happy until you bring it back into balance again. So what is your cause? What is your mission? What impassions you? Retirement doesn't have to mean apathy. Indeed, I believe retirement provides the opportunity for increased passion about life's purpose.

I'm not saying we're supposed to pursue a frenetic schedule of hourly events. Rest is fine. Go ahead and increase the amount of leisure over what you experienced during your working years. But don't put all your energy into leisure, because you'll quickly plumb those shallow depths.

## Our Developmental Path Brings Balance

As I've stated before, we move progressively closer to balancing the physical, the mental, and the spiritual areas of our earthly lives as we mature. To develop as God intended, we have to make the shift from bodily concerns to spiritual concerns. The primary shift occurs in middle age, when we stop measuring our life in terms of time since birth and begin measuring our life in terms of time until death. The shift can also come at other times, when dramatic life events wake us up and make us aware of how we need to reallocate our energy among the six life arenas.

This accumulation of experience in reallocating our life energy we call wisdom. Wisdom does a number of things. Here are four of them:

1. Wisdom gives us the power to weave the opposing factors of our lives into unity. Wisdom allows har-

mony to grow between our mind and our body, and
wisdom brings our mind from conflict to quiet fields
of peace.

2. At higher levels, wisdom allows us to reconcile our
   fundamental humanness and our essential spirituality. Wisdom lets us exchange the things of this
   world for the gifts of God, which are much more
   fulfilling and satisfying.

3. Wisdom allows us to unbind our minds from the
   trivia that has imprisoned us, to embrace the freedom of our primary dependence, and to place our
   total reliance on God.

4. Finally, wisdom bestows upon us the ability to recognize that what we thought was the pain, loss, and
   misery of aging is truly but another opportunity for
   learning how to love better.

Wisdom, the fruit of the maturation process, brings balance and wholeness, and with wholeness comes holiness.
What we call aging in the physical dimension is, in the spiritual dimension, the successive detachment from the material plane and a corresponding attachment to the things of
God. As Saint Paul advises, "Yet among the mature we do
speak wisdom, though it is not a wisdom of this age or of
the rulers of this age, who are doomed to perish. But we
speak God's wisdom, secret and hidden, which God de-
creed before the ages for our glory" (1 Corinthians 2:6–7).

Mature adults who achieve some level of balance are simultaneously infusing wisdom into their lives. Wisdom is
*the* virtue of maturation. Life balance and its consequence,
wisdom, allow us to understand Christ's promise to us in
ways heretofore unattainable. How many times have I heard

mature adults exclaiming with a sense of awe and wonder that they now understand the richness of a Christian life with vastly more depth and peace than they ever had before.

Life balance produces wisdom, and wisdom is a central ingredient of spiritual vitality. Christ wants us to live life to the fullest, but this does not mean that we live with abandon. We must appreciate life and gain a full measure of pleasure and abundance from life, as a wine connoisseur works to get the full measure of pleasure and abundance from wine. He or she strives with great gusto to balance all the senses, knowledge, and even spirit in such a way as to gain maximum appreciation. We live life best from a balanced perspective. It is here where we also find God.

# Epilogue

———

This book has simultaneously discussed the way to live agelessly and the way to live with spiritual vitality. At first, the two concepts may seem incompatible. One might seem to deal only with the physical body, the other only with the soul. But that is a shortsighted view. In stripping the body of its supple beauty, its graceful flexibility, its strong stamina, and its quick response, the process of aging, in the grand scheme of God's marvelous care, provides a magnificent opportunity for spiritual development. But we need to play our part well. If we wake up to what's really going on, we will come to know wholeness and holiness, despite our increasing physical and even mental limitations. In brief, we need to

- Adopt a new view of aging, a view compatible with the good news of love that Jesus teaches.
- Understand aging not as our enemy but as our master teacher helping us to learn how to love better each day.
- Recognize clearly that aging is part of God's plan for us, part of the eternal living water God promises.

When we close our eyes to worldly light and look instead within ourselves, we will discover the ageless wisdom of Christ and the awesome reality of God's love.

Here is the promise of aging, the hope of aging, and the mercy of aging.

# How to Personalize This Book

The author has developed an assessment questionnaire called *The Ageless in the Lord Profile* (ALP), which determines the degree to which you have already incorporated the 12 keys to spiritual vitality into your life, and quantitatively identifies those keys that may require more focused attention on your part. The 120-item questionnaire addresses the 12 keys in a new and inspirational way; it is an innovative creation based on the best principles of psychological wellness and spiritual wholeness.

The senior stages of our life span are designed by God as self-enhancing, not self-depleting. The ALP brings a new vision of abundance to these stages, helping us perceive and utilize the changes that later life brings in ways that enrich rather than diminish.

The ALP is specially recommended for both "renewal stage" adults, usually aged fifty to seventy-five, and "elder life" adults, aged seventy-five and over. For the renewal stage, the ALP serves as an anticipatory experience, assisting people in preparing for their own later years and in better understanding persons older than themselves. The ALP is particularly useful for elder life adults, those folks who may require a new definition of their own life stage that offers them rejuvenated spiritual growth and personal satisfaction.

The ALP is grace-filled, allowing senior adults of all ages to grow closer to God, closer to their real selves, closer to their God-centeredness by recognizing that aging is not what they thought it was...it is so much more!

Renewal stage and senior life adults might also benefit from attending any number of the author's "Ageless in the Lord" Seminars offered around the country.

Instructor certification courses, both in person and home study, are available; they provide certification as an "Ageless in the Lord Specialist."

Information on any of the above can be obtained from

The Association for Lifelong Adult Ministry (ALAM)
1714 Big Horn Basin, C-3
Wildwood (St. Louis), MO 63011-4819
phone (636) 273-6898
fax (636) 273-6899
Web site: SeniorAdultMinistry.com

# Index

# About the Author

R ichard P. Johnson holds a doctorate in gerontological counseling. He has worked extensively with religious groups across the United States and Canada, helping them to grow more vibrantly in the middle and later phases of their lives. He is the former director of Behavioral Sciences in the Department of Family Practice at St. John's Mercy Medical Center in St. Louis, Missouri. Currently, Dr. Johnson is executive director of the Association for Lifelong Adult Ministry (ALAM), located in St. Louis. His books include *Body, Mind, Spirit; Creating a Successful Retirement: Finding Peace and Purpose; All My Days: A Personal Life Review; How to Honor Your Aging Parents: Fundamental Principles of Caregiving;* and *Loving for a Lifetime: Six Essentials for a Happy, Healthy, and Holy Marriage.* He lives in Wildwood, Missouri.

# Other Titles from Richard Johnson

## All My Days
### *A Personal Life Review*

What greater gift could there be for senior adults than delving into the special moments, memories, and traditions that have shaped and enriched their lives? This personal journal provides a way for seniors to use their individuality and creativity in writing an account of their important and meaningful life events.

ISBN 978-0-7648-0643-8

## Loving for a Lifetime
### *6 Essentials for a Happy, Healthy, and Holy Marriage*

*Loving for a Lifetime* will help spouses identify their gifts, shadows, and compulsions, guiding them to a new sense of togetherness based on respect and communication. This strengthened relationship will bring a new sense of intimacy, deeper trust, lasting commitment.

ISBN 978-0-7648-0820-3

## How to Honor Your Aging Parents
### *Fundamental Principles of Caregiving*

Too often, people enter the role of caregiver for an aging parent unprepared, and, as a result of exhaustion, exasperation, and guilt, fail in their objective. These are not bad, lazy, negligent people. Most of the time, they simply tried to do too much. Written for any person who is caregiving or who anticipates that they will be called upon to give some form of care to an elder, this book sets out to prepare caregivers to do the best job possible to truly honor their aging parent, relative, or friend and yet not lose themselves in the process.

ISBN 978-0-7648-0476-2

*For prices and ordering information,*
*call us toll free at 800-325-9521*
*or visit our Web site, www.liguori.org.*